KU-200-838

WITHDRAWN

7 NOV 2010

Cambridge Wizard Student Guide

Hamlet
By William Shakespeare

THE LEARNING CENTRE
HAMMERSMITH AND WEST
LONDON COLLEGE
GLIDDON ROAD
LONDON W14 9BL

Kilian McNamara

B.A., Dip.Ed., Grad.Dip.Curriculum

CAMBRIDGE
UNIVERSITY PRESS

HAMMERSMITH WEST LONDON COLLEGE

328196

CAMBRIDGE UNIVERSITY PRESS
Cambridge, New York, Melbourne, Madrid, Cape Town, Singapore, São Paulo

Cambridge University Press
477 Williamstown Road, Port Melbourne, VIC 3207, Australia

www.cambridge.edu.au
Information on this title: www.cambridge.edu.au/0521536731

© Cambridge University Press 2005

First published by Wizard Books 1997
New edition by Cambridge University Press 2003
Reprinted 2005

Cover design by Cressaid Media
Cover art by Jon Crawley
Typeset by Aja Bongiorno
Printed in Australia by Print Impressions

HAMMERSMITH AND WEST
LONDON COLLEGE
LEARNING CENTRE

2 7 NOV 2008

328 96 £3-95
822.33 HAM MCN
LITERATURE
BWKS

National Library of Australia Cataloguing in Publication data
    McNamara, Kilian, 1952–.
    Hamlet.
    For VCE students.
    ISBN-10 0-521-53673-1 paperback
    1. Shakespeare, William, 1564–1616. Hamlet.
    I. Title. (Series: Cambridge Wizard students guide).
822.33

ISBN-10 0-521-53673-1 paperback

Reproduction and Communication for educational purposes
The Australian *Copyright Act 1968* (the Act) allows a maximum of
one chapter or 10% of the pages of this publication, whichever is the greater,
to be reproduced and/or communicated by any educational institution
for its educational purposes provided that the educational institution
(or the body that administers it) has given a remuneration notice to
Copyright Agency Limited (CAL) under the Act.

For details of the CAL licence for educational institutions contact:

Copyright Agency Limited
Level 19, 157 Liverpool Street
Sydney NSW 2000
Telephone: (02) 9394 7600
Facsimile: (02) 9394 7601
Email: info@copyright.com.au

Reproduction and Communication for other purposes
Except as permitted under the Act (for example a fair dealing for the
purposes of study, research, criticism or review) no part of this publication
may be reproduced, stored in a retrieval system, communicated or
transmitted in any form or by any means without prior written permission.
All inquiries should be made to the publisher at the address above.

Cambridge University Press has no responsibility for
the persistence or accuracy of URLs for external or
third-party internet websites referred to in this publication
and does not guarantee that any content on such
websites is, or will remain, accurate or appropriate.

Contents

The Life of William Shakespeare

William Shakespeare is regarded as possibly the greatest writer who ever lived. His works are known throughout the world, and are still performed constantly centuries after his death. Ben Jonson, the great Renaissance playwright and poet, and a contemporary, summed up Shakespeare's timeless gifts in a famous line: 'He was not of an age but for all time'.

Shakespeare's importance

The evidence of his genius is not hard to find. In a professional career of just over twenty years (c.1591-1612), he composed thirty-seven full length plays, plus three epic poems and 154 sonnets. Other writers have written more works, but none has produced so many masterpieces. Shakespeare is known everywhere for such immortal works as *Romeo and Juliet, A Midsummer Night's Dream, Much Ado About Nothing, The Merchant of Venice, Julius Caesar, Twelfth Night, Hamlet, Othello, King Lear, Macbeth, Antony and Cleopatra* and *The Tempest* – to mention just some famous titles. All his works have been tirelessly performed over four centuries, made into films, adapted into musicals and operas, and of course studied at length in schools and universities, not just in English-speaking countries, but, translated, in other places as well. This Renaissance genius is arguably the greatest name in European literature.

Childhood and education

He was born on 23 April, 1564, in Stratford, a small town about 160 km north west of London. John Shakespeare, his father, was a well-to-do businessman; his mother, Mary Arden, was the daughter of a prosperous landowner. He had a comfortable childhood, and received a good education (by the standards of the time) at the Stratford grammar school, learning Latin, literature, rhetoric, logic, science and mathematics.

Marriage

After leaving school, it is likely that he worked for his father. At the age of eighteen, he married Anne Hathaway, a young woman (of twenty-six) from a neighbouring village. She bore him a daughter, Susanna, and later twins, Judith and Hamnet.

By the time he was 23, however, Will Shakespeare had decided that country life was not for him. We may speculate that he had become intrigued with the idea of a theatrical career. Travelling players had certainly visited Stratford during Will's childhood, and in the year he left Stratford, no less than five acting companies had been in the town. Whatever the reason, in 1587 he moved to London. The reign of Elizabeth I was at its glorious peak and England was prosperous. Commerce and the arts were flourishing. The capital was full of writers, painters, architects, and wealthy merchants. It was one of the great centres of Europe, and the right place for a brilliant young man to find his destiny.

The move to London

Soon, he had managed to join the Chamberlain's Men (an acting company named after their patron, the Lord Chamberlain to Queen Elizabeth). He most certainly was an actor, though rapidly he demonstrated an astonishing gift for writing as well. At first he may have just adapted existing scripts, but by the time he was twenty-four he had begun writing his own original material. By the age of thirty, he had written the celebrated *Romeo and Juliet* (his tenth play).

Acting and writing

As a playwright, he was a huge success. He helped build the fortunes of the company, and was rewarded with both money and glory. In 1596, he was named a 'Gentleman' by the Queen (a fan of his work), and granted a personal coat of arms. By 1599 he was part owner of the company's own theatre, the Globe.

Success

When Queen Elizabeth died (in 1601), and James I became monarch, Shakespeare's company was taken up by the new king, and became the King's Men. More masterpieces followed, including his four great tragedies (*Othello, King Lear, Macbeth, Antony and Cleopatra*) and the immortal comic fantasy *The Tempest*. Eventually, having written at breakneck pace for over twenty years, and made a large amount of money, he retired to Stratford. He died on 23 April, 1616, and was buried in the local churchyard.

Great works

Death

In 1622, a collection of his works was published by his friends as a memorial to his work. This so-called *Quarto* edition was based on the best copies of scripts remaining. The following year, a more painstaking edition (the *First Folio*) was published. The latter is the major source of current working texts, including the one you will be using.

Posthumous editions

Shakespeare's Theatre and *Hamlet*

The theatre for which Shakespeare wrote was very different from modern theatre. A few words of explanation are necessary.

Before theatres

Permanent theatre buildings were a very recent development in Shakespeare's time. For centuries, actors had travelled around, like circus performers. The first theatre was not even built (in London) until 1576. It was modelled on the old innyard venues familiar to touring players: a rectangular courtyard, with a stage

The Globe theatre

coming out from one wall, roofed to keep the actors dry. Surrounding the stage were several levels of balconies, in which the patrons could stand or sit to watch the performance. The most famous of these theatres was doubtless the Globe, the venue of the Chamberlain's Men (Shakespeare's own company). It was a vast wooden building in Southwark, southwest of London Bridge, built in 1597. It was circular in shape, with an inner courtyard (open to the sky) into which jutted a central stage, which was itself roofed. Entrance was by a single door in the outer wall opposite the stage. It may have held up to one thousand people at a time.

Performances

Performances were always in daytime – so that the audience could see clearly what was happening on the stage. The poorest in the audience paid a penny and stood in the courtyard or pit around the stage. More well-to-do patrons could afford to buy seats in the tiers. The higher the tier the more expensive the seats. In Jacobean times (the reign of King James), indoor theatres began to appear. Other venues, more like the enclosed theatres of our own time, with candle lighting, began to develop late in Shakespeare's time.

The repertoire

Elizabethan theatre was a rich mixture of old traditions and ingenious adaptations. The repertory (repeated) genres of the travelling players were kept, because they were known to work. However it was now impossible to recycle the same works endlessly. New plays had to be written, and because the theatre was so popular, changed over rapidly. That is one of the explanations for Shakespeare's remarkable output (an average of two full length plays a year). Since the audience was a conglomeration of very different people, from the educated

Variety of styles aristocracy to the illiterate, plays attempted to offer something for everyone: sophisticated language and linguistic subtlety for the highbrows, a rollicking good story, often with bawdy humour, murder and fights for the 'groundlings' (the poor forced to stand on the ground in front of the stage throughout the performances).

Male actors Theatre was a sort of mass medium of its time. The companies were all male affairs, with boys taking the female roles (dressed as women and using their unbroken voices to sound 'feminine').

Bare stage The staging was still bare (by modern standards), with simple hand props and costumes, but no sets.

Origins of the play As with Shakespeare's other great plays, the story of *Hamlet* was not of his own invention. It was a traditional tale, of quite ancient origins.

Accounts of the revenge exacted by a prince against his murdering uncle go back certainly to the Icelandic saga of Amlodi, and probably beyond, to earlier Celtic or even Persian sources. It is highly likely that the real 'Amleth' was a local prince in Jutland in the seventh century (AD). Early versions of the story have the prince pretending to be crazy ('Amlothi' means crazy person), killing the wicked uncle, and eventually marrying and being killed

Early versions in battle. However, variants of the saga circulated. In the twelfth century, it was retold in the *Historia Danica* (Danish History) of Saxo Grammaticus. The central character became Amlethus. Claudius (Feng in Grammaticus' version), Gertrude (Gerutha) and the other characters are all visible under different names.

Over the next several centuries, the story spread throughout Europe. In 1576, it reappeared in a slightly modified form, in the *Histoires Tragiques* (Tragic Stories) of François de Belleforest. In the Belleforest *Hamlet*, the Queen (Gertrude) had been involved in an adulterous affair with her brother-in-law (Claudius), which goes some

Kyd's Hamlet way to explain Hamlet's disgust at his mother. Probably based on this source, and probably written by Thomas Kyd (author of the famous *Spanish Tragedy*), an English version of the story was performed in London in the early 1590s. This version, called by scholars the *Ur-Hamlet*, is now lost. It added the ghost, a favourite device from the

Shakespeare's Roman writer Seneca, Kyd's inspiration. It is thought that this *Hamlet*

Hamlet was a property of the Chamberlain's Men, performed a number of times, and that Shakespeare reworked the story, from the Kyd version, in 1600 or 1601. We believe that Shakespeare himself played the part of the ghost in his own *Hamlet*, when it was first performed.

Notes on Genre, Structure and Style

Hamlet is a **verse drama**, and generically, an **Elizabethan revenge tragedy**. Approaching a work of literature is always made easier by some sense of its context, and this is never more crucial than with a text that is four centuries old. Let us examine its generic characteristics one by one.

Revenge stories

Firstly, it is a revenge story. The Elizabethans loved 'blood and guts' tales, the equivalent of our own enthusiasm for horror stories. When the story could be given a satisfying moral twist, such as 'the mutability of fortune and the just punishment of God in revenge of a vicious and evil life' (a summing up of what tragedy offered audiences by Greville, a contemporary of Shakespeare's), so much the better. There were indeed a whole series of so-called 'revenge tragedies' during the late sixteenth century.

Why revenge?

The theme of revenge was popular in Elizabethan tragedy because it touched on important questions of the day: the moral and social problems of personal honour and the survival of feudal lawlessness; the political problem of tyranny and resistance; and the supreme question of providence, with its provocative contrasts between human vengeance and divine.

Moral issues in revenge tragedies

Bad things were always being done to people. In extreme cases (as in *Hamlet*), we are talking of murder and treason. How should they react? With Christian forbearance, or with bloody savagery? The latter, which usually led to heaps of bodies on the stage, was enormously exciting to audiences in Shakespeare's time (as horror stories still are today). Morality was not offended, however, because the person taking the bloody revenge was himself killed off too – thus demonstrating the Biblical canon, 'Vengeance is mine [ie. the privilege of God alone], I will repay, saith the Lord'.

The Spanish Tragedy

The earliest significant Elizabethan revenge tragedy was *The Spanish Tragedy* (1592) by Thomas Kyd (1558-94). It was really what we would now call melodrama (ie. a tale of stereotyped characters, exaggerated emotions and unlikely plots), but it was hugely popular. It is oddly like *Hamlet* in some respects, though not in quality. A young man, Horatio, is treacherously killed by two scheming villains just as he exchanges vows of love with his young lady. His father swears to seek vengeance. Feigning madness, and a little mad with grief anyway, he contrives to have a play performed at the wedding of the villain. At the wedding, revenge and murder are unloosed; all involved are killed. Kyd had learnt the crowd-pleasing effect of horror from studying the work of the Roman writer Seneca. Tricks like ghosts, tales of bestial behaviour, passionate speeches and epic bloodshed proved highly attractive to audiences, and the success of *The Spanish Tragedy* started a craze for other revenge tales. Also in this vein were Marlowe's *The Jew of Malta* (1589), Marston's *Antonio's Revenge* (1599), Tourneur's *The Revenger's Tragedy* (1606) and others. Most of the other revenge tragedies of the time were little more than 'blood and guts' sagas, with thin characterisation, but wild scenes of emotion and lots of violence.

Other revenge plays

*Why **Hamlet** is different*

Hamlet is different. It does give its audience plenty of stimulation – a ghost, two murders, madness (real and simulated), swordfights, poison, a mountain of corpses – but it also offers us one of the most complex characters ever put on stage, and moral dilemmas of great subtlety. We cannot and should not ignore the revenge aspects, treating the violence as some sort of mistake on Shakespeare's part – that is part of what makes it great theatre and enduringly popular – but we should also see that there is much more to this brilliant work of literature.

Tragedy

Secondly, the text is a *tragedy*. There is no doubt about this: the word is on the title page. These days, the word is used loosely to refer to anything very sad, such as an untimely death or other personal disaster. However, Shakespeare's use of the term has a more theoretical basis. He was knowingly working within the conventions of an ancient dramatic form which goes right back to the ancient Greeks. When they wrote tragedies, they were following a very specific narrative model. The definitive explanation of classical tragedy comes from Aristotle (384-322 BC). He described it as:

Aristotle

Quote

an imitation [fictional account] of an action [set of events] that is serious, complete, and of a certain magnitude [grand, lofty]; in language embellished with each kind of artistic ornament [poetic, rich]...though pity and fear effecting the proper purgation of these emotions.

(from *The Poetics*)

So a tragedy is a story richly and artistically told, of pitiable, fearful events, which should deeply affect the viewer, but at the end leave him/her emotionally whole again. The Greek word *katharsis* [purgation] is often used in literary discussion to describe what Aristotle meant here: that by identifying with characters in crisis, a reader/viewer is engaged in a powerful response, and by this process deals safely with these emotions (since it is not a real but simulated involvement), and 'gets it out of his/her system'. Aristotle goes on to describe the central character in a tragedy:

The use of tragedy

Quote

The change of fortune [or terrible decline which is the basic action] must not be the spectacle of a virtuous man brought from prosperity to adversity: for this moves neither pity nor fear; it merely shocks us. Nor, again, that of a bad man passing from adversity to prosperity…[for that is morally repugnant]. [But it should concern] a man who is not eminently good and just, yet whose misfortune is brought about not by vice or depravity, but by some error or frailty.

Hamartia

In short, a tragic hero must be both good *and* bad – so that we to some extent identify with him (though shrinking from what he does) and learn from the experience. In Aristotle's view, the tragic hero must possess an *hamartia* [tragic flaw], which brings him down. We sympathise with him, while also regretting the flaw which turns out to be fatal. The story thus works out a moral argument: this flaw is to blame; look what it has done!

The tragic hero

It is necessary to understand the Aristotelian model of tragedy because it is important in *Hamlet*. Tragedy shows us the fatal tendency of people to let their weaknesses undermine their strengths. The mix of admirable and destructive in human nature is the whole point. If Hamlet were just a saintly man, who followed the Biblical commandment to 'turn the other cheek' and forgive (his murdering uncle and his adulterous mother), we would have no story. If he were a simple-minded butcher, who, immediately he heard what Claudius had done, went out and killed him on the spot, we would have a crude revenge tale, and little else. Certainly, there would be not much to admire in Hamlet. In fact, we have a clever balance of both alternatives: a man who has no wish to kill, but cannot abide the dishonour and grief of doing nothing. Hamlet's noble and sensitive nature struggles against the dark urges within him throughout the play. His pride will not let him rest, but his indecisive nature will not allow him to act. There has been long and confusing debate about what stops Hamlet from acting, but his 'tragic flaw' is central to the way the play works.

Hamlet: a verse drama

Lastly, let us consider what is one of the most striking aspects of this drama from a modern point of view. It is not written in ordinary speech, but in verse. Why? Because rich language, heavily ornamented with metaphor and worked into metricated (regular, though not generally rhymed) lines was considered artistic, and faithful to the long tradition of theatre that had come down to the Elizabethans from ancient Greece and Rome. Consider the following lines from *Hamlet*:

> Quote
>
> O that this too too sullied flesh would melt,
> Thaw, and resolve itself into a dew....

Iambic pentameter

What do you notice? That each line has exactly ten syllables? That the stress falls (usually) on the second beat in every pair? If you did, you picked up the two main technical features of what is called *iambic pentameter* – iambic referring to the alternating soft-hard beat and pentameter to the five syllables in each line – the preferred verse form of Shakespearean drama. This is usually called 'blank verse' (blank denoting the absence of rhyme). It is important to understand that a typical Shakespearean drama is not just an exciting story, but *poetry*. Attending to the play of words, the figurative language and the allusions is essential to a full response to the text.

Prose speeches

At other more 'prosaic' moments in the play straight prose is employed. Whenever announcements are to be made, orders given, Shakespeare often reverts to prose. It is also used as a social marker, as when Hamlet addresses his social inferiors, such as the players (Act 3, Scene 2), or when people of limited social standing (sailors and gravediggers) make speeches. In other words blank verse, the 'poetry' of the play, is given a privileged status befitting those of noble rank, those whose minds presumably move on loftier planes. Prose is also used at times when Hamlet is playing at being mad, again indicating that 'poetic' lines are for moments of serious discourse. By these devices does Shakespeare signpost the play for us.

It will obvious from these remarks that Shakespearean drama does not attempt to be 'naturalistic' (life-like), in the manner of many modern plays, and most popular film and television. Not only do the characters speak in verse, but they think aloud, address the audience directly, and spell out their motives in a way which can seem remarkably direct for contemporary audiences. Hamlet for instance repeatedly tells the audience (in asides) what he is thinking. Whole soliloquies (solo speeches) are devoted to his moral agony. Why this convention? Partly that Shakespeare had no conception of 'realism' (the idea that art should pretend to exactly mimic real life). Partly to make things plain to the audience. They were watching a live performance in a large theatre. They could not see facial expressions well: certainly close ups were out of the question. They had to work out who was who, where the action was taking place and what everyone's motives almost entirely from the words given to the characters. So Hamlet's soliloquies are externalising his motivation in a very neat way which far from offending anyone's expectations would have made his character that much clearer.

Soliloquies

We are studying the printed text of a work of early seventeenth century verse drama. We must see the text as a drama (ie. story of conflict designed to be performed live), we must pay attention to its qualities as poetry, and we must try to see how it expresses its meaning and works its artistry within the theatrical conventions of the period (as explained above). To dismiss the text because it is not like a modern play, or because the language is 'difficult', is like sneering at a Victorian mansion because it does not have central heating or automatic doors. Bear with the initial difficulties of reading Shakespeare. They pass. The story is powerful, the art is remarkable, and you can be confident that you are studying one of the great works of world literature.

Summary and Commentary on the Text

ACT ONE

Scene 1

The watch

Francisco (a soldier) is on sentry duty. Bernardo (an officer) enters, together with Horatio (a friend of Hamlet), and Marcellus (another officer). Horatio has been asked by Marcellus to share the watch this night, on account of a **'dreaded sight twice seen'** by Marcellus and Bernardo.

The ghost

Barely has Bernardo begun his story, when a ghost appears. It takes the shape of Hamlet, the late king. Bernardo and Marcellus urge Horatio to address the ghost, but it disappears.

Marcellus questions Horatio about the preparations for war everywhere to be seen. Horatio replies that Fortinbras, Prince of Norway, is planning to recover the lands lost by his father in an earlier conflict with the late king of Denmark (old Hamlet). Bernardo

Ill omens

believes that **'this portentous figure'**(the ghost) may be an omen of further strife between the nations. Horatio is more troubled still, fearing that it is a portent (or sign) of great evil about to befall Denmark, similar to those grim portents that preceded the death of mighty Caesar in Rome.

The ghost reappears

The ghost reappears, and Horatio demands that it speak to him. There is no reply and, on the cock's crowing for dawn, it once more fades from sight. Horatio suggests that **'this spirit, dumb to us'** will doubtless speak to Hamlet.

Commentary Note the swift economy with which Shakespeare sets the tone of conflict and doom. Not only is a restless ghost in the shape of the dead king stalking the battlements, but celestial **'harbingers'** of **'feared events'** have been seen in Denmark of late. What's more, war is expected at any time.

This cosmic symbolism is not mere theatrical atmosphere. The Elizabethans believed in the notion of God's universe as a kind of seamless garment, in which no part was isolated from any other. Evil could not simply do its worst, without any 'symptom' appearing. We think of the night of Duncan's murder in *Macbeth* and how all of nature seemed to rise up in fearful protest against that dark deed. Similar supernatural occurrences are now evident – begging the question 'What is wrong?' and (by implication) who has committed what act to provoke such ominous signs?

The ghost is clearly a focal point for all this. It is also a brilliant dramatic device, calculated to send chills running down the necks of the audience. However, not only does it give no message. We are not even sure it can be trusted. The cock which crows at dawn banishes it from sight. Can any of its utterances be taken at face value? Or is it in league with the 'Prince of Liars'? The opening scene asks more questions than it answers. A 'mystery' is set before us (who is the ghost and what does he want), which we know will lead to deep and darker things, yet to be revealed.

Scene 2

Claudius talks of war

Claudius (the King) enters, with his court. He is at pains to justify his recent marriage to Gertrude, widow of the late king. It was with a heavy heart, he declares, that he and the grieving widow joined together in marriage, to unite Denmark at a time of great peril. Besieged from without by Fortinbras, and imperilled from within by the dangers of a nation left without a king, Denmark needs his firm leadership. He commands Cornelius and Voltimand to carry tidings to Norway, uncle to Fortinbras, reminding him that revenue for the armies of Fortinbras will empty his own coffers.

Laertes

Claudius then turns to a request by Laertes that, having visited Denmark to dutifully acknowledge Claudius' accession to the throne, he should now return to his studies in Paris. Claudius refers the matter to Polonius, Laertes' father and the Lord Chamberlain. The request is speedily granted.

Hamlet's troubles

In far less cordial tones, Claudius now turns his attention to the 'clouds' troubling young Hamlet, 'my son'. Gertrude begs Hamlet to cast off his melancholy, to refrain from seeking forever his **'noble father in the dust'**. She reminds him that death is common and that **'all that live must die'**. Claudius commends him for his filial piety, but argues that any period of mourning indulged beyond a decent interval displays **'impious stubbornness'** and **'unmanly grief'**. He urges Hamlet to look upon him as a father. He makes clear his desire that Hamlet should not return to Wittenberg to study. When Gertrude adds her voice to this request, Hamlet agrees to stay. All go, leaving Hamlet alone.

Commentary The first point to note is the absolute political mastery of Claudius. Alternating between a kind of bullying joviality and imperious grandiloquence, he is never less than completely in command. Quickly he glosses over any misgivings which his court audience might have concerning the speed with which he has taken Gertrude as his wife. Quickly he binds the nobility of the court of Denmark to this expeditious marriage (they have 'freely gone/ With this affair along'). We might also note the exaggerated courtesies extended to Polonius, father of Laertes, upon his son's request to leave for France. We wonder if *his* loyalty has been purchased at some cost. Furthermore, he is no slouch when it comes to statecraft. Far from a disunited kingdom following the death of old Hamlet, Fortinbras must now face a wily foe, ready to undermine his demands with a clever mercenary appeal to his Uncle, and source of funds, old Norway.

Having deftly handled these affairs of state, Claudius moves on with equal skill to Hamlet. Quick to perceive the kind of nuisance which a grieving, suspicious son might be at court, he seeks to bind him to his new family loyalties. Hamlet is reminded that he is virtually a son to the new king. **'A little more than kin, and less than kind'**, mocks Hamlet in his first witty aside. Claudius has become a 'little more than kin' (he has moved even closer to Hamlet by becoming his stepfather or kindred), and yet he is still less than 'kind'. Related he may be to Hamlet, but he lacks the virtues associated with 'kith and kin', such as loving and brotherly concern. The first pall of suspicion is now cast upon Claudius. We are drawn into a kind of stage-managed alliance with Hamlet, privy to his thoughts in a way the other players are not.

While managing to conceal his contempt for Claudius, for his mother Hamlet has nothing but open scorn. His retort, in the face of her entreaties to be reasonable and forget about his late father, is utterly scathing. He contrasts his own genuine grief with his mother's seeming *lack* of it. She has abandoned her period of mourning with indecent haste, and stands condemned for her indifference.

Hamlet's first soliloquy

Left alone, Hamlet launches into the first of his famous soliloquies. Entreating heaven that this **'too too solid flesh would melt'**, and bitterly regretting God's decree against suicide, he rails against the world. How **'weary, stale, flat and unprofitable'** seem to be all its **'uses'**, he says. The world is a corrupt, evil place, an **'unweeded garden'**, in which things **'rank and gross in nature'** triumph, while decent mortals pass away. His noble father has been succeeded by a 'satyr' (in mythology, half man half goat), and most disillusioning of all, his own mother has, with **'wicked speed'**, taken to her **'incestuous sheet'** (the marriage bed), her father's own brother. She is now revealed to Hamlet as coarse in nature, her seeming love for his late father all too fallible.

Commentary This soliloquy is one of the most famous in all of Shakespeare. It begins with an impassioned plea that this 'too too solid flesh would melt'. Much scholarly debate has centred around the adjective which begins the speech. Some scholars have argued that Shakespeare originally wrote 'sullied', not 'solid' and indeed it appears in a number of editions of the play. The distinction does open up interesting possibilities. If his flesh is indeed too 'solid', then a plea that it should 'melt' could be seen as a prayer for a speedy death. If it were to 'melt' then he would not have to wreak grievous harm upon it. It would simply melt away, freeing his soul from torment, and himself from the need to 'self-slaughter'.

However, if the flesh of Hamlet is 'sullied', there is also room for interesting speculation. It recalls the biblical use of the term 'flesh' – a portmanteau term for all the weakness and frailty to which humans are subject – and implies that his 'flesh' is not only weak and subject to human temptation, it is also tainted. He has recognised the contagion of human existence. He can no longer consider himself above the fray; he is down there in the muck with the rest of humankind. Hence the prayer that this 'too too sullied flesh' should melt. He wants no part of it. He cannot abide even thinking about the kind of moral carelessness which allows his own mother to quickly throw off the trappings of grief and enter the marriage bed with her late husband's brother. Nor can he stomach the ease with which those who are most 'sullied' should flourish in this world. His is the abiding torment of the sensitive soul, the pain of those whose moral sense is exquisitely attuned to any wrongdoing. For Hamlet there is nothing left but a kind of existential *angst* which seems peculiarly modern in its expression. His railing against the 'weary, stale, flat, and unprofitable ...uses of this world' could have come quite easily from any twentieth century text.

We become conscious of an unpleasant sexism in the play, an attitude towards women typical of earlier periods of history when patriarchal attitudes held sway. For, in condemning his mother for her hypocrisy and sexual greed, he comes perilously close to the old prejudice which linked all female 'flesh' with that which is most corrupt and corrupting. His cry, **'frailty, thy name is woman'**, goes much farther than a simple diatribe at the expense of 'weak' women. Rather, women in general constitute that 'flesh' that he would like to see melt. In their very bodies, in their creative sexuality, they partake of the very corrupting weakness which 'pure' men must avoid at all costs. We are not far from the poisonous misogyny of the Church fathers and a celibate clergy which for centuries kept women in bondage. This distrust and fear of women will later curse his relationship with Ophelia, as she is a part of that tempting but dangerous 'flesh' of which he must be rid. Why this pathological distrust of women? He has been betrayed at the core. The mother whom he has most trusted, most loved, has 'betrayed' him, made 'incestuous' alliance with another man. There is much more at work here than the Christian proscription against marrying the sibling of a dead spouse. A Freudian interpretation would see Hamlet as suffering from an unresolved Oedipal conflict (see Theme notes). He cannot have his mother, and no other man will either.

Already we are gleaning valuable insights into the character of Hamlet and deeply disturbing they are! He seems to oscillate between a cynical wit (such as the comment about the cold meats at his father's funeral serving well at the marriage table), and a kind of melancholy, suicidal depression. 'What's the point of it all?' sums up the latter mood. He seems a man entirely unsuited to action. A kind of monastic contemplation of the world's 'uses' and abuses would serve him better. He is too warmly, too passionately engaged to want death, in reality, but he seems too highly strung, to take effective action.

Horatio tells
Hamlet of the
ghost

Horatio, Marcellus and Bernardo appear. Horatio informs Hamlet that a ghost resembling his late father has been spotted three nights in a row on the ramparts of Elsinore. Hamlet questions them closely about the appearance of this ghost and vows that he will join them tonight in watching out for this apparition, even if 'hell itself should gape' at his impudence in so doing.

Commentary In the closing moments of this scene we glimpse a more robust Hamlet, ready to meet the ghostly apparition so like his father. Great must be his appetite for further knowledge, for he is prepared to risk damning his soul by confronting this spectre. In the Protestant theology of Shakespeare's time the prevailing orthodoxy was that such ghosts were 'angels' or 'devils'. If the latter, they could assume the likeness of one's near departed in order to tempt one into damnation. Hence his bold assertion that hell itself will 'gape' at the confrontation. The problematical nature of this ghost and any of his utterances is becoming one of the central conundrums of the play.

Scene 3

Laertes and
Ophelia

Laertes is about to depart for France. He seeks to warn his sister, Ophelia, about the ephemeral nature of Hamlet's affections, which are **'not permanent, sweet, not lasting'**. He may say that he loves Ophelia, but **'his will is not his own'** when it comes to matters of state. Laertes urges his sister not to allow her 'chaste treasure' to be wantonly spent.

Laertes departs

Ophelia chides her brother for its self-evident hypocrisy. Laertes should not, she says, dispense wisdom about the 'steep and thorny way to heaven' and then play the libertine himself.

Polonius enters. After a lengthy dissertation on manners, morality and being true to oneself, he farewells Laertes. Laertes reminds Ophelia once more of his words of warning and Ophelia promises to heed them.

Polonius and
Ophelia

Polonius then questions Ophelia as to the substance of that conversation, and Ophelia informs him. Polonius tries to disillusion his daughter about men's affections. Ophelia is just **'a green girl'**, and Hamlet's offerings are not **'sterling'**, he says. Ophelia protests that, in all his dealings with her, Hamlet has acted in an **'honourable fashion'**. Polonius replies that these vows of Hamlet spring more from lust than love. At first he urges her to spend less time with

Hamlet and to play harder to get. Finally, he commands that she have no more words with the young man. Ophelia agrees to do as he says.

Commentary In this scene we come to a clearer understanding of what Laertes and Polonius are really like. Both pontificate to the submissive Ophelia, ostensibly for her benefit, but actually betraying more about their own natures. In both the libertine (promiscuous) Laertes and the pompous Polonius the sexual hypocrisy of the patriarch is unmasked. In such families, the brother carries on the duty of the father to warn, to counsel and to control. In the father's absence the son will assume the role of *paterfamilias.* They will not admit that what is good for the gander is also good for the goose. In their dire warnings about Hamlet and his evil intent they are unwittingly exposing themselves. They are saying in effect that Hamlet is not be trusted *because* he is a man. They know how untrustworthy is their nature. By extension, all men must be the same.

Are they genuinely concerned for Ophelia's well being, or for rigid patriarchal notions of honour, and female obedience? Their control of her is to have dire consequences later. Forbidden to see Ophelia, Hamlet's disillusionment and distrust of women can only grow. Ophelia is now set on the road to misery (and eventual madness), as she seeks to repress her natural feelings of affection and desire for Hamlet. Polonius is exposed as a tyrant on the home front who lacks wisdom and perception. He would rather trot out hackneyed advice about young men and what they get up to, than come to know his daughter. We know that on the political stage he can readily play courtier to the new king. We suspect that he is a hollow man, and perhaps a devious one into the bargain.

Scene 4

Hamlet awaits the ghost

Hamlet, Horatio and Marcellus are on the castle battlements. Within the castle can be heard the sounds of revelry. Hamlet remarks that this is customary in Denmark, but is a custom he would gladly see abandoned, since it taints the national reputation. He goes on to observe that **'the stamp of one defect'** can mar a man's reputation even if he is otherwise blameless.

The ghost appears. Horatio and Marcellus beg Hamlet not to

The ghost appears

follow the ghost, but he will not be deterred. The value of his life is naught, he declares, and his immortal soul cannot be endangered by one equally immaterial. Horatio warns that the ghost may 'assume some other horrible form' and then tempt Hamlet to suicide. Horatio and Marcellus try to physically restrain Hamlet, but he will not be swayed. As he follows the ghost, Marcellus swears that **'Something is rotten in the state of Denmark'**.

Commentary What do we make of Hamlet's critical remarks about the carousing within the castle? Is it just resentment at Claudius and his delight in sensual pleasures? Or is it the same kind of metaphysical disgust at the indulgence of worldly 'flesh' which he manifested in the first soliloquy, the sign of extreme moral fastidiousness?

It is most telling that Hamlet should brood, so early in the play, on what he calls the **'particular fault'** (for which one might read 'fatal flaw') which can sully a man's reputation, and (by implication) lead to his downfall. Although he speaks as it were in general, his words could well apply to Claudius (whom he has already accused of being lustful and greedy) and even more intriguingly, perhaps without knowing it, to – himself. By Hamlet's account, the 'stamp of one defect' may not be of a man's own doing; it may simply be that **'nature's livery or fortune's star'** has visited a single defect upon an otherwise blameless character. We are reminded that in the Elizabethan era there was a widespread belief in astrology and the idea that life was controlled by the planets, the stars and their constellations. The 'defect' issue reminds us of the idea of the 'tragic flaw' which brings down otherwise noble characters in both Greek and Shakespearian tragedy. If Hamlet's remarks could be taken to include himself, what might be the nature of *his* 'fatal flaw'?

Of interest to us as well is the perception of Horatio that this phantasm may unhinge Hamlet's mind. The very fact that Horatio is so quick to jump to this extreme conclusion suggests that perhaps Hamlet's mental stability is the subject of some gossip at Elsinore. It is not simply Claudius and Gertrude who are aware of the 'toys of desperation' which cloud his reasoning.

The closing words of Marcellus, 'Something is rotten in the state of Denmark', recall Hamlet's own words that the world is an 'unweeded garden', in which all manner of things 'rank and gross in nature' flourish unhindered. We know that this corrupt, scheming world is one in which Claudius is most at home. We wonder at the mettle of Hamlet and how well suited he is to the kind of spirited action needed to overthrow such men.

Scene 5

The ghost's story

The ghost tells Hamlet that he is the spirit of his father, doomed to purgatory. He calls upon Hamlet to revenge his **'foul and unnatural murder'**. The story about how he died (of snake bite), was a lie. The 'serpent' is none other than Claudius. While he slept, his brother poured a fatal poison into his ear. He had no time to receive the last sacraments, and thus suffers the fires of purgatory.

Old Hamlet begs his son not to allow the **'royal bed of Denmark'** to be **'a couch for luxury and damned incest'**, yet also pleads that any revenge should spare Gertrude. Her judgement will come later in heaven. He bids Hamlet adieu, saying, **'Remember me'**.

Hamlet vows revenge

Hamlet vows that he will wipe away all other thoughts and memories from his mind, save revenge of his father's untimely death. He curses his mother (**'O most pernicious woman!'**), and the **'smiling, damned villain'** who is Claudius.

Hamlet swears his friends to silence

When Horatio and Marcellus appear, Hamlet will say nothing of what the ghost revealed. He makes them pledge never to reveal what they have seen. They are offended. From below a voice cries: 'Swear!' Horatio seems dumbfounded by these happenings, but is reassured by Hamlet that **'There are more things in heaven and earth than are dreamt of in your philosophy.'** Hamlet orders them to remain silent in the face of whatever 'madness' he may decide to feign in future. It may suit his purposes to **'put an antic disposition on'** and they must not, by word or deed, link it in any way to this night's strange happenings. For Hamlet it seems that **'the time is out of joint'**, and if he was born to set it right then he is indeed cursed.

Commentary With this scene we come to a critical development in the story. For in the ghost's revelation we have the beginnings of the principal narrative – Hamlet vows revenge the revenge drama. Hamlet's father has been murdered, and he has set the young man the task of avenging his death. The rest of the play is dominated by this challenge. Hamlet may have accepted the necessity of despatching the wicked brother, Claudius, but it will not be an easy thing to achieve. Besides, there is still the possibility that the ghost is not *really* his father, but a spirit sent to trick Hamlet.

We must bear in mind that Hamlet is being called upon to avenge himself upon a king. To contemplate toppling such a man or, even worse, taking his life was no small matter. Hence it is doubly important that the truth of this matter be worked out here on earth. Even if the ghost is the spirit of the dead king, his story, and the truth of his identity, are not yet confirmed. If he is not what he claims to be, if he is simply another manifestation of the Devil himself, then the call to regicide is a call to Hamlet's damnation. The ghost, not Claudius, would be the real 'serpent', the same one who lured the original couple into sin (Satan).

This scene also foreshadows the much debated nature of Hamlet's madness. We should pay careful attention to Hamlet's words at this point. Troubled he may be, maddened by the conflicting pressures he must handle. But in his dealings with Horatio and Marcellus, there is no doubt that an 'antic disposition' (pretence of madness) is something that he plans to 'put on'. Behind the cloak of insanity he may be able to flush out the truth of this matter more easily than if he were to assume the potentially hazardous role of court inquisitor.

In the closing scenes of this act the stage has now been set for the conflicts to follow. We see in Hamlet a man in many ways unaccustomed to the demands of political battle. He seems uncertain, lacking the mettle to take on the task which has been set him. He seems to oscillate between a fevered excitement at the prospect of avenging his dead father, and a near paralysing hesitancy at the thought of action. Part of this quandary arises from the uncertain nature of the ghost and hence the dangers in answering his call for revenge. Partly it arises from Hamlet's own doubt-ridden nature.

ACT 2

Scene 1

Polonius is sending his servant Reynaldo off to Paris with letters and money for Laertes. He asks Reynaldo to make inquiries about his son.

Ophelia appears, claiming that she has been 'affrighted'. Lord

Ophelia tells of 'mad' Hamlet

Hamlet, his garments unkempt and his manner wild, entered her room with a **'look so hideous in purport'** that it seemed that he had just been **'loosed from hell'**. Polonius wonders if Hamlet is suffering the madness of love. Ophelia is unsure, but fearful. She tells of how Hamlet held her at arm's length, regarding her with a steely gaze and nodding three times as though something he had long suspected was indeed confirmed.

Polonius convinced it is love

Polonius asks her to accompany him to the king. Polonius sees this as **'the very ecstasy of love'** which unhinges reason. He wonders if Ophelia has **'given him** [Hamlet] **any hard words of late'**. She reminds Polonius that she has obeyed his wishes and denied Hamlet any access to her. Polonius believes that this is what has made Hamlet mad, and asks forgiveness in making what was evidently a foolish judgement.

Commentary Our attention in this scene is focussed on Ophelia's description of Hamlet. Is he merely feigning madness, or showing signs of genuine instability?

His earlier assertion that he would 'put an antic disposition on' sits oddly with Ophelia's description of his behaviour. There is no evidence of grief at his father's death in his bizarre confrontation with Ophelia, or signs of his wider plan. Rather, it seems that the earlier obsessions with women and their 'frailty' have now resurfaced. Not knowing of Polonius' foolish command against Ophelia seeing him, he can come to no other conclusion other than that another deceitful woman has betrayed him. His worst fears are confirmed as he gazes into her eyes. They are all betrayers, creatures of the flesh. This seems to be his unwarranted conclusion. We hearken back to his condemnation of his own mother, his disgust at her taking another man to her marriage bed. Now the full force of his disgust is about to be unleashed on the hapless Ophelia, who is clearly out of her depth in dealing with him.

Is Hamlet simply assuming the cloak of madness? We recall his earlier erratic behaviour at the ghostly presence beneath the stage as he swore both Marcellus and Horatio to secrecy. Our doubts about the sanity of Hamlet are now very real. Whatever the truth, we suspect that nothing good can come of this new twist.

Scene 2

Before Claudius stand two boyhood friends of Hamlet, Rosencrantz and Guildenstern. Claudius refers to Hamlet's 'transformation' and suggests they may be able to draw him out. They readily agree.

Polonius' news   Polonius now enters with the news that the ambassadors to Norway have returned. In addition, he assures Claudius that he has found **'the very cause of Hamlet's lunacy'**. Gertrude makes plain to Claudius that in her mind the cause of her son's unrest is **'his father's death'** and their **'o'erhasty marriage'**.

Voltimand appears, saying that the King of Norway has suppressed the war plans of Fortinbras. This pleases Claudius greatly. The ambassadors depart.

Polonius then announces that Hamlet is mad, telling Gertrude and Claudius that the cause is his daughter. He quotes at length from a love letter, and admits that it was he, Polonius, who ended their budding courtship. Gertrude and Claudius both admit that this is a plausible explanation for Hamlet's condition. Polonius tells them that they may hear for themselves what kinds of mad utterances are made in the presence of Ophelia.

Hamlet acts   Hamlet enters. He greets Polonius as a 'fishmonger', and warns
the madman   him not to let his daughter walk in the sun for fear that she might conceive. Polonius switches the subject to the 'matter' of Hamlet's reading. When asked what is the matter (the substance), of his reading, Hamlet wonders what the 'matter' is, and who is troubled by it. He says that the book is about old men and that it is full of 'slanders'. Polonius admits in an aside that 'Though this be madness, yet there is method in't'. When he is gone, Hamlet dismisses Polonius as one of these 'tedious old fools'.

Hamlet,   Rosencrantz and Guildenstern enter. Hamlet makes great verbal
Rosencrantz and play about the notion of Fortune (fate), and wonders what brings
Guildenstern   them to this 'prison' which is Denmark. They protest. The discussion shifts to Hamlet's **'bad dreams'** and how, for Hamlet, a dream is 'but a shadow' of reality.

Hamlet comes to the nub of the problem. Have they come of their own accord to visit an old friend, or were they sent for by other parties? Rosencrantz and Guildenstern admit that they were sent for.

The discussion turns to the imminent arrival of a group of players [actors], whom Rosencrantz and Guildenstern overtook on the road to Elsinore. Rosencrantz reminds Hamlet that he was once inclined 'to take delight' in the plays offered by these 'tragedians'. Hamlet warns his two friends not to be deceived: he is only **mad 'north-north-west'**; when 'the wind is southerly', **he knows 'a hawk from a handsaw'**.

Commentary Hamlet's 'transformation' is the major subject of this scene. Polonius offers his theory, a sort of comic relief, all the funnier because Polonius is so serious about it. More perceptive is Gertrude, who correctly intuits that it was the old king's death and her too hasty remarriage which have unsettled Hamlet's mind.

In the scene where Polonius quizzes Hamlet, we see a much more playful side to the prince's nature. The apparently crazy description of old Polonius as a 'fishmonger' (Elizabethan slang for a pimp), in fact makes excellent sense: it fits what we have learned about him. He would gladly prostitute his own daughter ('loose' her), if he thought it would advance his cause before the King. Less delightful are the references to Ophelia, likening her flesh to that of a dead dog, able to 'breed maggots' in the noonday sun. Hamlet seems utterly convinced that she is not to be trusted, that she is a willing part of all that 'too too sullied flesh' which can only make 'good kissing carrion'. Any fruits borne of such a sexual union can only be corrupt, Hamlet implies, further hardening our suspicions that for Hamlet all women have been tainted by 'original sin'.

In this scene, the celebrated matter of Hamlet's thinking becomes an explicit issue. He utters the now famous line, **'There is nothing either good or bad, but thinking makes it so'**. Such a comment appears to admit that his sour perception of the world may well be the product of a disordered mind. But at the same time he offers the utterly modern perception that there is no objective truth outside our *perception* of it. He can on one hand acclaim 'the beauty of the world', while at the same time lamenting its corruption. It's all in the mind, says Hamlet, and the workings of his own mind seem as much a mystery to him as they are to us. His state of depressed inactivity, his wavering between melancholia and frenetic urgency, are a symptom of this mental confusion.

But is he *mad*? Leaving aside the pantomime quality of the

encounters with Polonius, he is absolutely astute in his comments. Polonius' observation that if 'this be madness, yet there is method in't' is more astute than he knows. We actually hear from Hamlet's very lips that those who think him mad are 'deceived'. All his erratic behaviour is nothing but show, designed to trick Claudius into some admission of his guilt.

Hamlet and the players   Once more Polonius enters, to announce that the players are now at Elsinore. The players appear and are greeted by Hamlet. He calls upon them to recite some lines from a play he remembers, about the death of Priam (king of Troy). The story is taken up by one of the players. Hamlet asks the players to stage a play tomorrow, *The Murder of Gonzago*, into which he wishes to insert some lines of his own.

Commentary   With the arrival of the players, we are reminded of the idea of a shadow-play, of the deceptive nature of appearances and how difficult it is to perceive the truth. The earlier remark about 'something rotten' in the state of Denmark now has another possible meaning. Not only is there the matter of the secret murder, but of the prevailing duplicitousness of the court. What is rotten, what eats away at the body politic, is that *nothing is what it seems*. Claudius is not the noble, concerned fatherly king he wishes to appear. He is a murderer. Gertrude is far from being the concerned maternal figure she seems. His friends are not his friends, but spies. It is a state full of pretence, in which sycophantic courtiers have 'freely gone with this affair along'. Faced with such murderous deceits, Hamlet too must take refuge in pretence. Denmark is full of people playing parts, while the unsavoury truth lurks beneath their adopted masks.

Hamlet's second soliloquy   Now left alone, Hamlet soliloquises again. He ponders how a player can conjure up the tears and heartbroken emotions appropriate to a character's fate, simply by force of his imagination. How much more then should he, Hamlet, who has every reason to feel impassioned, act with purpose and dispatch in a matter where his duty is clear? He must be every kind of **'ass'**, lacking in courage, to be so fatally indecisive when his father's murderer goes unavenged. He can manage only empty words when heaven calls out for bloody vengeance on the culprit.

He resolves to catch Claudius out through *The Murder of*

Hamlet's plan to expose the King   *Gonzago*. He has heard that guilty parties, upon seeing their sins enacted on stage, have confessed to their evil deeds on the spot. Perhaps Claudius will be similarly afflicted with guilt and admit to his crime. Hamlet is still worried that the spirit with whom he has spoken may be the devil in human guise, leading Hamlet to his damnation. The play will be the vehicle for establishing the truth of the matter.

Commentary   Hamlet's second soliloquy offers key insights into his character. Why does he damn himself so? The source of that conflict lies in Renaissance ideas of the 'parfit [perfect, ideal] knight' and how *he* should behave, contrasted with Christian ideals of passivity and acceptance of harm by others (the willingness to 'turn the other cheek', no matter what).

These quite separate ideas are blatantly self-contradictory and perhaps Hamlet cannot be blamed for his failure to reconcile them! The honour code of the knight compelled him to take up arms against those who would besmirch his honour. Hamlet is well aware of this tradition. In its terms, he has failed, and is as low as a **'peasant slave'** (one at the very bottom of the feudal order), the wretch who seeks only to save his own life, no matter what compromise that involves. The noble knight, by contrast, is meant to fight to the death for his honour. If dishonour could not be avoided, then suicide was the next best alternative. We must be mindful of this at all times whenever Hamlet ponders 'self-slaughter'. It is not some coward's way out he is seeking, but the second best alternative if he cannot avenge the dishonour against his father.

On the other hand, as a Christian he should *forgive* his uncle and his mother, and learn to live in peace with them. Revenge and killing have no place in the moral scheme of things associated with the teachings of Jesus. Hamlet is caught on the horns of this dilemma. Should he follow the chivalric code of honour and kill Claudius, or the religious call to sanctity and forgive him? It may be of little interest to a modern day audience but this tension, this ambivalence, was deeply rooted in the culture of the times. Hamlet is but one of its many victims.

ACT 3

Scene 1

Rosencrantz and Guildenstern report back

The King is questioning Rosencrantz and Guildenstern about Hamlet. They suggest that he has assumed a **'crafty madness'**, with which he keeps himself aloof. They tell of Hamlet's joy at the arrival of the travelling players, and Polonius hastens to assure the king and queen of Hamlet's desire to see them at their coming performance. Claudius agrees to attend.

Polonius 'sets up' Ophelia

Claudius asks Gertrude to agree to Polonius' plan to spy upon Hamlet and Ophelia when they 'accidentally' meet. Gertrude agrees.

Polonius takes Ophelia aside, asking her to read from a holy book, with 'devotion's visage'. In an aside, Claudius admits that all this studied deception is playing on his conscience and that his **'deed'** (which he has glossed over with a 'painted word'), is proving to be a **'heavy burden'**.

Commentary This is a major revelation. For the first time Claudius admits that his conscience is troubled. Clearly he has not abandoned all moral sense, has not comfortably assumed the role of usurper to the throne. Moreover, he is also fearful for his own fate.

Hamlet's third soliloquy

Hamlet enters and begins perhaps the most famous soliloquy in all of Shakespeare's works, beginning **'To be or not to be'**. He ponders whether it is worth continuing to live, or whether it is simpler to die. Even to risk the dreams which might come in that **'sleep of death'** seems tempting. All it would take would be a 'bare bodkin' (dagger). Yet perhaps it is this fear of the evil which awaits them, the **'dread of something after death'** (Hell, in the case of a suicide), that holds men back from such an end and allows them to endure the **'calamity'** of a **'long life'**. It is this fear of suicide which makes **'cowards of us all'**.

Commentary In the 'To be or not to be' soliloquy, we confront, in all their complexity, the metaphysical problems which bedevil Hamlet. It has some echoes of the first soliloquy. In that, he called for this 'too too solid [or sullied] flesh' to melt away, to leave him incorporeal, freed of the world's trials and corruptions. However, as with the first soliloquy, we should be careful of an overly literal 'reading' of the text which sees it as all about toying with the idea of suicide. Rather it is a weighing up of moral imperatives, imperatives which pull him in seemingly contradictory directions, contradictions which of their very nature *cannot be resolved*.

Should he take the noble but passive road of Christian acceptance and **'suffer/ The slings and arrows of outrageous fortune'**? Should he turn the other cheek and, Christ-like, accept the blows which fall upon him? This is the call to Christian sanctity, of avoiding the sin of revenge. Hamlet sees himself in many ways as the 'parfit knight', and is loath to abandon this carefully cultivated self-image. As a perfect *Christian* gentleman, he should *not* kill, however much he is provoked.

However, the perfect gentleman is also the warrior duty-bound to retaliate against those who wrong him and bring his good name into disrepute. He is the one who will **'take arms against a sea of troubles'**, take the fight up with those who have wronged his father. That fight may even be an impossible one (fighting the very ocean waves). Yet it may be the good fight which *must* be fought. Interesting also is the use of the comparative adjective. There is no dispute that *both* courses of action are noble. The question is about which is **'nobler'**. This is from a man who sets himself very high ethical standards in a kingdom where double-dealing and deception have become the order of the day!

There are also the problems surrounding death and the way in which we reach our mortal destination. Again, we feel for Hamlet and his dilemma. If evil deeds went unavenged then choosing death by one's own hand was a way for the man of honour to expunge the stain upon the family name. But for a Christian, such a passage could only lead to that **'undiscover'd country from whose bourn/ No traveller returns'** (purgatory). It is the 'dread' of what lies beyond that keeps men in thrall to this **'weary life'** and which allows them to suffer all the degradation and toil of everyday existence, while others less worthy grow prosperous and contented.

Hamlet is held back, by temperament, doubt and moral fastidiousness, from taking violent action against those who would oppress him. Equally, he fears death by his own hand, mindful of the Christian ban on suicide. But his greatest fear is that he is drifting into a kind of moral vacuum. He is neither taking up arms, nor accepting his fate like some kind of saintly pacifist. The greatest danger is that he will continue to drift aimlessly, unable to break the cycle of apathy and inaction. In this melancholic torpor, moreover, he courts another sin – that of inactivity, of failing to act, the sin of omission. What he needs more than anything else is a kind of moral 'circuit breaker', something which will enable him to throw off his nervous indecision and take action, or at least settle into some kind of peaceful acceptance of what has occurred.

Hamlet and Ophelia

Ophelia enters. They talk, and he makes verbal plays upon the words **'honest'** (truthful, but also modest and chaste) and **'fair'** (white and, presumably, virginal). He tells her that beauty has the power to subvert honesty. Hamlet admits that he did once love her, but that he lied. He advises her to get to a 'nunnery', where she is less likely to be a 'breeder of sinners'. She should believe no men. They are all 'arrant knaves'. Hamlet unleashes a diatribe against women, and says it is better that she marries a fool, for **'wise men know well enough what monsters you make of them'**. Ophelia is shattered by Hamlet's words, believing that **'a noble mind is here o'erthrown'**.

Claudius will exile Hamlet

Polonius and Claudius re-enter. Claudius will entertain no more talk about love and the effect it has had on Hamlet. He is sure that there is **'something in his soul'** which is troubling Hamlet and is determined that Hamlet must depart for England. Perhaps the 'seas and countries different' will help to expel this **'something-settled matter in his heart'**. Polonius proposes that Gertrude take Hamlet into her confidence while Polonius listens in on their conversation. If this does not succeed they could then fall back on Claudius' plan. Claudius agrees.

Commentary What are we to make of the confrontation with Ophelia? Madness, or moral outrage? Claudius sums it up well. Hamlet's condition 'was not like madness'. He is however troubled. The irony of this insight (given Claudius' implication in that troubled state) is obvious.

Hamlet is disgusted at mankind. **'We are arrant Knaves all'**, he declares wretchedly. In telling Ophelia to get herself to a 'nunnery', he is saying that if she would be pure she must reject all men. He has seen that corruption is everywhere. Implied in this condemnation are all three men involved here: Claudius, a murderer and liar (what irony that Claudius is listening!); Polonius, a fool and deceiver (also listening); and Hamlet himself, a self-confessed 'coward' (as per the last soliloquy).

When she protests however, he lashes out at women too, and expands the idea of corruption effectively to everyone, male and female. Paradoxically, the word 'nunnery' puns with an Elizabethan slang word for a brothel (a 'nonnery'). Since Hamlet almost immediately attacks women in general,

> **Quote**
>
> You jig and amble, and you lisp; you nickname God's creatures and make your wantonness your ignorance.

a sneering critique of coquettish feminine behaviour, we see that such a suggestion could fit with his misogynistic contempt for women. He is no doubt thinking of his mother. But he has now added poor Ophelia to the list of corrupted individuals. Ophelia is caught in an impossible dilemma. No matter what form of words she comes up with, she cannot escape the verbal snares Hamlet has set for her, nor turn back his disgust.

Scene 2

Hamlet and the players

Hamlet is talking with the players, giving them instruction, so that their drama may **hold a 'mirror up to nature'**. Horatio enters, to be warmly greeted by Hamlet. He bids Horatio pay close attention to tonight's play, especially the scene which 'comes near the circumstance' of his father's death.

Hamlet awaits the play

The players enter, and the court. Hamlet is playful. He mocks Polonius and makes bawdy sport with Ophelia. Ophelia says that he looks 'merry', and he gaily asks what else can a man be in the face of the cheeriness of others. Look upon his own mother and how happy she is within hours of his father's death! Being reminded by Ophelia that his father is now two months dead, he sarcastically remarks that perhaps a dead man's memory has a chance of lasting half a year in the minds of those left behind.

The dumb show

At this point, the dumb show begins. A king and queen embrace, then the queen departs as the king lies down to sleep. A man comes in to pour poison into the ear of the sleeping king.

Finding the king dead upon her return, the queen mimes grief. The poisoner creeps in again, and comforts the grieving queen, wooing her with gifts. After a while, she accepts his protestations of love.

Asked by Ophelia the meaning of this little dramatic performance, Hamlet replies that it is **'miching mallecho'** (secret mischief). Ophelia is told that all will be explained.

The play-within-the-play

The play now shifts to a spoken form. The Player King warns the Player Queen that he is not long for this world and hopes that she will find as kind a husband as he. She declares that such a love would be 'treason'. Only a woman who killed her first husband could take a second, she says. The King seems pleased at this, but reminds her that there is a great gap between our present intentions and our final actions. Again she protests in loud tones that once a widow she would never be a wife. Hamlet asks Gertrude how she is enjoying the play and she replies that **'The lady doth protest too much'**. Claudius is finding the scene offensive, but Hamlet replies that it is all in 'jest'. He has named the play **'The Mouse-trap'**.

Claudius flees

Now poison is poured into the Player King's ear. Claudius rises and rushes from the scene. All depart, leaving only Hamlet and Horatio behind. Hamlet is overjoyed.

Commentary The opening moments of the scene are interesting in that they refer to Aristotle's mimetic theory of art, in which 'a mirror' is held up to nature. The quality of a performance (and art in general) is in other words to be judged by whether it achieves a 'realistic' portrayal of human life, especially human suffering. This in turn fits in with the larger literary context, for instance the Aristotelian theory that by vicarious experience of emotions (fear, grief, compassion) in responding to art, we are purged of those emotions, as well as being improved by the moral content of the work. The 'play within the play' is a fascinating example of how art, here dramatic art, works as a representation of human experience.

The dumb show, as well as the full play, showcase Shakespeare's skill in a memorable way. For we become conscious that here is a play about how plays work, which is not dully theoretical at all, but brim full of emotion and narrative implications. The drama of the 'Mousetrap' is framed within the drama of *Hamlet* – one set of actions (the Lucianus story) detonating reactions and radically shifting the dynamics of the larger story (Hamlet, Claudius et al). The 'metanarrative' (thinking about the story as a story) implications of this scene have exercised students and scholars for generations.

At last Hamlet gets the 'proof' he wanted. Claudius condemns himself beyond any doubt by his semi-hysterical reaction to the simulated murder (which so closely mimics his own real murder of his brother). And Hamlet's reaction in turn is one of sweet relief. For the ecstatic moment after his ruse succeeds, he ceases to doubt the ghost, and sees revenge as clear.

Hamlet rebuked Rosencrantz and Guildenstern appear, saying that Claudius is 'distempered' (angered) by this performance. After more idle banter, Hamlet agrees to go and see his mother, who according to Guildenstern is **'in most great affliction of spirit'**. When Rosencrantz begs Hamlet in the name of friendship to unburden himself, Hamlet refuses. All he will admit is that his wit (his mind), is diseased and that he lacks 'advancement'. When the players enter with recorders, Hamlet makes an analogy between playing on the instruments and Guildenstern lying and trying to 'play' him.

Gertrude calls Polonius reappears and is once more the butt of Hamlet's
for Hamlet barbed wit. Hamlet agrees to visit Gertrude but, left alone, utters darkly that it is now the 'witching time of night'. He prays that he will be able to contain his murderous impulses towards her and that though he may **'speak daggers to her'** he will, at least, **'use none'**.

Commentary Despite Hamlet's gleeful triumph upon the exit of Claudius, we are still unconvinced about his propensity for action. It is as though the symbolic unmasking of Claudius will substitute for the real thing. Is it sufficient that Claudius should retire to his bed 'distempered'? Hamlet seems to think so. Should he not also be charged with his crime and dealt with? Again, we wonder if *Claudius* is really the object of Hamlet's anger. Is it not Gertrude whom he seeks out at the end of this scene, barely able to contain his murderous impulses? Moreover we wonder if, for Hamlet, **'the play's the thing'**. Shadow play, simulacrum, rather than harsh reality of brutal action, suits this man of *inaction*.

Scene 3

The King is deep in conversation with Rosencrantz and Guildenstern. It will not stand 'safe with us' to let the madness of Hamlet 'range', he argues. Hamlet must be despatched to England without delay.

Polonius will spy on Hamlet

Once Rosencrantz and Guildenstern have gone, Polonius enters to inform Claudius that Hamlet is about to visit his mother's room. Polonius will hide there to overhear their conversation, as it will require someone less 'partial' than a mother to make a disinterested judgement on that exchange.

Claudius prays

Left alone, Claudius is filled with remorse. **'O! my offence is rank'**, he admits. Like the sin of the biblical Cain (who slew his brother Abel), this deed of his **'hath the primal curse upon't'**. He cannot pray for forgiveness, even though 'inclination be as sharp as will'. He thinks of the mercy of God. Was it not meant for sinners like himself? No sooner has he consoled himself with this thought than he remembers that there can be no forgiveness while he is still possessed of the fruits of his evil deed (**'my crown, mine own ambition, and my queen'**). There will be no 'shuffling' (bribery) permitted there. There the sin will be revealed in its 'true nature'.

Hamlet's dilemma – kill Claudius at prayer?

He kneels to pray, and it is thus that Hamlet finds him. Tempted to kill him on the spot, Hamlet still hesitates. Why should he kill this murderer and assure his soul of a quick flight to heaven? His own father was taken 'full of bread' (with his own sins unrepented), and so dwells in purgatory, his sins as yet unatoned. Better, surely, to take him when he is 'drunk asleep', or 'in the incestuous pleasures of his bed', or in the thick of some other action that will ensure his soul be **'damn'd and black'**. His mother awaits him. This revenge can wait for a choicer moment.

Claudius gets to his feet, realising that all efforts at penitence are wasted. His words may 'fly up' to heaven, but his 'thoughts remain below'. For as long as this is the case there can be no genuine contrition.

Commentary In this scene we see a completely new side to Claudius. An all too human side to the man is revealed. His prayers are genuine. Hamlet only accidentally stumbles across him. Claudius seems to be genuinely tormented. He is fearful that his soul is now doomed and yet unwilling to give up the spoils of victory. He also has the decency to admit that his heart is not in it. He will not mutter pious words of contrition until there is genuine remorse and a genuine wish to repent.

What of Hamlet's reaction? Is it the rather vindictive (though understandable) argument that it would be better to catch Claudius out at a time when he is enjoying the pleasures of the flesh, rather than in a moment of repentance which stops his hand? Or is it yet another hesitation, the problem that '**conscience** [thinking] **does make cowards of us all**'? Hamlet will not receive a better chance to take his revenge upon Claudius.

Scene 4

Polonius advises Gertrude to warn Hamlet that his 'pranks' must cease. Meanwhile he will hide himself and await Hamlet.

Hamlet and Gertrude

Hamlet enters the queen's chamber. On hearing Gertrude's reproach that he has '**thy father much offended**', Hamlet neatly turns the verbal tables. She has his father 'much offended', Hamlet retorts, referring to his blood father, not his father by marriage. She accuses him of speaking with an '**idle**' tongue; he accuses her of speaking with a '**wicked**' one. Upon being asked whether he has 'forgotten' her, he replies in tones of bitter contempt that he cannot forget that she is his mother, although he wishes it were otherwise. Nor will he let her go, but demands that they sit together while he holds up a mirror to her 'inmost part'.

Hamlet kills Polonius

Gertrude calls out, begging not to be murdered. Hearing her cries, Polonius also calls out from behind the tapestry. Hamlet leaps up and stabs with his sword through the cloth. Reproached by Gertrude for this '**rash and bloody deed**', Hamlet retorts that it is almost as bad as killing a king and marrying his brother. Finding the dead Polonius behind the arras, Hamlet is cold and unmoved. Polonius is a '**wretched … intruding fool**' whom he mistook for his 'better' (Claudius).

Hamlet chastises his mother

He demands that Gertrude admit her wrong-doing. She cannot use the excuse of love, argues Hamlet, for the hot blood of passion is now 'tame' in one her age. She now lies in her 'enseamed' (sweaty, dirty), bed, '**stewed in corruption, honeying and making love**'. Gertrude cannot bear this tirade of abuse and begs Hamlet to desist. His words are like 'daggers'.

At this point the ghost enters the room. Although Hamlet addresses him, the ghost is invisible to Gertrude. She calls Hamlet

The ghost recalls Hamlet to his duty 'mad' for talking to the thin air. Hamlet wonders whether his ghostly father has come to chide him for letting such a long time lapse without firm action. The ghost replies that he has indeed come to **'whet'** that **'almost blunted purpose'**, but also advises Hamlet to speak to his mother, as she is filled with 'amazement' (surprise and fear). Hamlet further admonishes her. Meanwhile the ghost steals away.

Hamlet counsels Gertrude Hamlet tells her that if she wishes to embark on the road to virtue she should refrain from visiting her husband's bed tonight. As for the death of Polonius, he regrets what occurred, but it is heaven's wish that now he must be God's 'scourge and minister'. **'I must be cruel only to be kind'**. Hamlet advises her to keep up the pretence of affection for the king, concealing from Claudius that Hamlet is not so much mad as crafty. He reminds his mother that he is now bound to go to England. The body of Polonius he carts away as he bids his mother good night.

Commentary Hamlet's moral crusade is here brought to a type of completion. He confronts Gertrude about her sins and she admits them. Yet the scene is not an easy one. Many readers over the years have had real trouble with the extremity of Hamlet's disgust at his mother. He takes a kind of delight in describing the intimate details of her squalid affair with Claudius. Is this the sign of a rank and disordered imagination, a sexual obsession, misogyny (the sacred image of the virgin mother replaced by this nightmarish vision of a whore), even a Freudian problem? Or is it a proper dramatic expression for the depths of horror he feels at what is quasi-incest, as well as his mother sleeping with her husband's killer?

The capitulation of his mother seems however to purge him of the many demons which have so troubled him. His manner towards his mother shifts from one of moral disgust to an almost patronising concern. For her part she seems like putty in his hands once she has admitted her wrongdoing.

Again, we are puzzled by the changes which have overtaken Hamlet. Earlier we have witnessed his torment as he wrestles with his conscience, goaded to action, yet petrified by uncertainty. He has missed his golden opportunity to have revenge on Claudius (III. iii), yet now seems curiously content to drag away the body of an old man who offered him no physical threat. It can only be surmised that Polonius has come, in his mind, to join those who conspired with the new king to usher in the new order. All of them, loyal courtiers, flatterers, Polonius, Rosencrantz and Guildenstern, are all tarred with the same brush. Now that he has (accidentally) killed one of them, a great load seems to have lifted off Hamlet. They have become mere bodies to be dispatched. He has become heaven's 'scourge and minister' and has all the self-assurance, even complacency, that comes with divine appointment.

Act 4

Scene 1

Gertrude pretends Hamlet is mad

Claudius confronts Gertrude about her troubled condition. She confesses to Claudius that Hamlet, mad 'as the sea and wind', has killed Polonius. Claudius tells her that Hamlet's 'liberty' is now a threat to them all. He and Gertrude must now with all their 'majesty and skill' try to cover up and excuse this crime.

Rosencrantz and Guildenstern are recalled and told to move the body of Polonius to the chapel. Meanwhile Claudius and Gertrude will speak to loyal friends and advisers and seek to gloss over this sad affair, so that no whiff of scandal fall upon them.

Commentary Safely out of the clutches of her son, Gertrude seems once more the loyal wife of the king. Nevertheless she keeps up the fiction, if fiction it be, that he is mad rather than 'crafty'. Although her confession to her son seemed at the time merely a tactical concession, her failure to inform Claudius is a clear sign of some allegiance between herself and Hamlet. If mad, Hamlet can be dismissed. If sane, he is a danger, and this she pointedly fails to mention to Claudius.

Of Claudius we note how quickly he gathers his wits, how speedily he moves to cover up this latest crime so that it may be readily explained away, no taint of guilt to be attached to him.

Scene 2

Rosencrantz and Guildenstern confront Hamlet. Regarding the whereabouts of Polonius' body he will only say that he has

Hamlet refuses to co-operate 'Compounded it to dust' (buried it). Hamlet blasts his former friends as sycophants of the king who will be dispensed with when no longer needed.

Commentary Hamlet toys with the courtiers with the self-assurance of a man set on his course, a kind of devil-may-care determination to see the matter through. The banter with Rosencrantz and Guildenstern – the jest about where the body is buried, the quip about Polonius being with the king (the dead one) – is comic relief perhaps, but also the sign of a man released from uncertainty, no longer tormented by self-doubt or frozen in the apathy of grief.

Scene 3

Claudius now confesses that Hamlet can no longer go loose. Yet they cannot 'put the strong law on him', for he is much beloved by the 'distracted multitude'. He must be sent away.

Hamlet arrested Hamlet is brought in under guard. To the king's query concerning the whereabouts of Polonius, Hamlet will only answer that he is at 'supper' – not where he eats, but where he is eaten (by worms). Hamlet informs him that Polonius is either in heaven or 'i the other place'. He thens jokes about finding him within a month with their noses.

Hamlet banished Claudius informs Hamlet that his grievous action must spell banishment, if only for his own safety. When Hamlet is gone, Claudius prays that if he has any influence at all in England, then the letters, once opened, should seal Hamlet's fate.

Commentary There is a malicious glee in Hamlet that is very attractive at times. And this is one of those times. How frantic is Claudius to glean information from Hamlet so that this whole unseemly business can be smoothed over. And how flippant is Hamlet with his part-theological, part-biological discourse on the fate which awaits us all. Behind the whimsy, however, is the deadly serious intent of this young man, the kind of world-weary disillusionment which enlivened his first soliloquy – a sense of mortality and grief at man's lot. At times like this there is an almost existential despair about Hamlet that seems quintessentially modern.

Hamlet, after vacillations and confusion, is now alert and focussed. Not for a second is he fooled by the false mask of goodwill and concern for his safety and well-being. He knows this is all a plot to end his life. And how confident he seems, assured in his new-found role as an angel of vengeance. Either he will emerge unscathed from these encounters, or he will die. He seems singularly unconcerned for his fate.

Scene 4

On a plain in Denmark we encounter Fortinbras and his soldiers, seeking safe passage as promised. When they leave, Hamlet, Rosencrantz and Guildenstern enter.

Hamlet's fourth soliloquy

Begging to be left alone, Hamlet begins his fourth and last soliloquy, in which he makes bitter commentary once more on his lack of action. Every occasion seems to further condemn his failure to act, his **'dull revenge'**. What is a man if his only purpose is to 'sleep and feed'? Such a man is little more than a 'beast', an insult to his maker who gave him **'capability and god-like reason'**. These faculties should not be allowed to atrophy through disuse. Was it **'Bestial oblivion'** on his part, or some **'craven scruple'**, perhaps **'thinking too precisely on the event'**, that has held him back from decisive action? Still the task lies ahead of him and he cannot deny that he has the **'cause and will and strength and means'** to do it. He should look to the example of Fortinbras, who is willing to go to war over such a trifling matter as this parcel of land when *'honour's at the stake'*. How does *he* stand as a man of principle, with **'a father kill'd, a mother stain'd'**? From this moment forth, he swears, his **'thoughts [will] be bloody'** or they are worth nothing.

Commentary Once more in this scene we revisit the notion of chivalry or courtly 'honour'. Fortinbras is held up by Hamlet as the very model of a man of action. He will go into battle, fight to the death over a piece of territory, take up arms against an enemy, if he perceives that family or national 'honour' has been besmirched. How much further, then, should Hamlet go, whose very house has been dishonoured by a vile murder and sinful marriage? Hamlet is galled by the contrast between the determined Fortinbras and his own wavering resolve. He is trying still to strengthen his commitment to action. So often have we seen him chide himself for tardiness, for failure to act decisively, that we are not sure how seriously to take him this time. If we do take him at his word then, indeed, he may be capable of the kind of bloodthirsty performance he so admires in Fortinbras. If not, he will remain the indecisive Hamlet we have come to know.

Scene 5

Ophelia has gone mad

Gertrude, Horatio and a gentleman are discussing the piteous state into which Ophelia has sunk. She speaks 'much of her father' and seems quite mad. Gertrude is distressed. She allows the gentleman to bring Ophelia to her. While waiting for Ophelia she confesses her overwhelming sense of guilt.

Ophelia enters but does not recognise Gertrude. Instead she starts singing little ditties. One is a song of lament in which the abandoned lover wonders how she will know her true love, as he is 'dead and gone'. The king enters at this point, but can get no more sense out of her. Ophelia now sings about Saint Valentine's day and a maid who went to her lover's house only to emerge a maid no more. That maid feels deceived as she would not have consented to losing her virginity but for his promise of marriage. Ophelia continues her diatribe (in which can be gleaned a good deal of sense). She rues the loss of him laid 'i the cold ground'. Her brother Laertes will be informed of all this, she mutters to the assembled company. She goes.

Claudius speculates that it is the loss of her father which has spurred such grief. How unwise they were to so quickly and secretively bury old Polonius. The people of Denmark are now agog with rumours. Ophelia is **'Divided from herself'**. Worst of all, her brother Laertes has returned from France and, lacking substantial information, will think nothing of pointing the finger of guilt at Claudius for his late father's death.

Laertes returns

A gentleman enters to inform Claudius that Laertes has mustered a riotous crowd, ready to overthrow Claudius and install *him* as king. Laertes bursts in and demands of Claudius that he hand over his father. Claudius reminds him of the divine right of kings. He tells Laertes that his father is dead, and that he (Claudius) is **'guiltless'**.

Laertes and Ophelia

Ophelia comes back in. Laertes, perceiving immediately that his sister has lost her mind, is distraught. Ophelia sings about her late father's funeral. Claudius urges Laertes to go find his 'wisest friends', who will attest that he, Claudius, had nothing to do with the death of Polonius. If still dissatisfied, Laertes may claim the entire kingdom, the throne and all that is theirs.

Commentary It is more than the death of her father which has affected Ophelia. Her songs are not simply about bereavement. They are also about betrayal. Given that there is no evidence of a physical love between her and Hamlet, we can only speculate that Hamlet's cavalier treatment of Ophelia, and the constant references to her whoring nature, associated in her imagination with a complete loss of honour and abandonment, have unhinged her mind. She now believes that he had his way with her, becoming, in her own mind the wretched 'fallen woman' of song and folklore. Thus far gone in madness, she cannot see how she may have played a part in his condemnation of her, how *her* abandoning *him* at least temporarily unsettled *his* mind. She was simply acting on her father's orders, like any dutiful daughter. All memory of how she was instructed to accept no more compliments from the young man has been erased. It is a tragic state indeed!

What are we to make of the contrast between Laertes and Hamlet! Is Laertes the consummate man of action, quick to take action against the wrongdoer (though he has the wrong man in this case)? Or is he a hot-headed fool, and Hamlet the noble man who has refused to act with unseemly haste. Is Laertes good to seek revenge, or hasty and of doubtful character? This is exactly the moral problem Hamlet had when he sought the right course of action earlier.

Scene 6

News of Hamlet Horatio speaks with sailors who show Horatio a letter written by Hamlet. It tells of his adventures at sea and how they were pursued by pirates. After some fighting between both crews, Hamlet leapt aboard the pirate ship, which then moved away, effectively imprisoning him on board. The pirates have treated him well, however, and they have promised to lead Horatio to where Hamlet is hiding. Rosencrantz and Guildenstern are still on their way to England.

Scene 7

Claudius plots with Laertes

Claudius persuades Laertes of his innocence and, furthermore, convinces him that Hamlet now seeks the life of the king. Claudius argues that he cannot readily take action against Hamlet because of Gertrude, as well as the public esteem in which Hamlet is held. Claudius assures Laertes that he will have his revenge.

A messenger arrives, with a letter from Hamlet. It informs him that Hamlet will return 'naked' (unarmed), the next day to give an account of himself.

The duel plot

Laertes says he looks forward to meeting Hamlet face to face and accusing him of the dastardly deed. Claudius then makes Laertes promise to his go along with his plan, which will entail no hint of wrongdoing on their part, whose outcome will seem an 'accident'. Upon Hamlet's return, Claudius will set up a fencing duel between them. Hamlet will be easily duped into choosing a conventional fencing sword, while Laertes picks a sharply pointed one. Not to be outdone, Laertes proposes that he will coat its tip with poison, thus ensuring Hamlet's fate. Claudius further proposes that he will prepare a poisonous potion such that when drinks are called for, Hamlet will drink from the 'chalice' and die.

Ophelia dead

Gertrude enters to tell Laertes that his sister has drowned. The news arouses in Laertes another bout of fury. He goes, followed by Claudius and Gertrude.

Commentary Claudius continues to reveal himself as a wily manipulator. His apparently moderate remarks about not being too hard on Hamlet are hardly genuine. He is trying to deflect the rage of Laertes. What of the scheme to have Laertes dispatch Hamlet? What of his ready acquiescence in the poisoned sword trick? Claudius is not a monster, but he is an undoubted villain.

Act 5

Scene 1

The graveyard scene

The scene is a churchyard. Two grave diggers, dressed as clowns, are talking about Ophelia. Why is she to be buried with full Christian rites, since she so 'wilfully' sought 'her own salvation' (ie. suicide).

Horatio and Hamlet enter at a distance and watch. The first

clown orders the second to fetch him some liquor while he sings a ditty about youthful love and the earthly grave which awaits us all. Hamlet is quite taken aback at this merriment. He observes how the grave digger plays with the bones he has dug up as if they were 'loggets' (skittles). Hamlet engages in some verbal sparring with the clown until he finally admits that it is a woman for whom this grave is being prepared.

Hamlet and 'Yorick'

Hamlet falls into a kind of sorrowful reverie as the grave digger shows him another skull. This one belonged to Yorick, the old king's jester. Hamlet remembers him well, 'a fellow of infinite jest'. He ponders again life's cruel ironies.

Funeral of Ophelia

A funeral party enters, with Laertes, the king and queen and mourners. They carry the corpse of Ophelia. Hamlet immediately senses that the 'maimed rites' (foreshortened ritual) indicate a death by suicide.

Laertes questions the priest about the brief service and is informed that she cannot expect a full Christian burial. Hamlet suddenly realises that it is Ophelia over whom these prayers are being said. Gertrude strews flowers over the bier, wishing that it was her bridal bed she could bedeck with flowers (on account of her marriage to Hamlet). The very mention of the name Hamlet sends Laertes into another frenzied rage. He leaps into the grave to embrace his dead sister once more. Not to be outdone, Hamlet also leaps in, declaiming his love for Ophelia to be as great, if not greater, than any brother.

Hamlet fights Laertes

Laertes now grapples with Hamlet, cursing him wildly. They are separated. Hamlet continues to assert that, such were his feeling for Ophelia, 'forty thousand brothers' could not match his love. Furthermore he is quite willing to fight Laertes over this issue.

Hamlet goes out. The king urges Laertes to have patience. They will soon have their chance to test the 'love' of Hamlet in a duel.

Commentary The interchanges between Hamlet and the gravediggers/clowns is partly a comic interlude, but its subject matter, however jokingly treated, is of greater significance. It is part of the recurrent musings on mortality by Hamlet. The reference to Cain is fairly obvious. Here lies a skull that might have belonged to the first man who murdered his own brother – the biblical Cain. That other fratricide (Claudius' slaying of Hamlet's father) is never far from his thoughts and, increasingly, the death of its perpetrator preoccupies him. He seems obsessed with life's cruelties and ironies. Where are the quips and jests of those who would clown around? Where are the fine words of lawyers, of emperors, of world conquerors even? What do we take with us? In *Hamlet*, we are confronted not just with the specifics of individual deaths (that of the old king, of Polonius, and now Ophelia), we are reminded of the ever-present shadow of mortality itself.

> **Quote**
>
> Now get you to my lady's chamber, and tell her, let her paint an inch thick, to this favour [a skull] she must come.

Hamlet's melancholia is not just temporary derangement. It is the age-old angst of knowing the end of the human condition.

By a savage irony, Hamlet's musings on death are now given an even sharper edge. Ophelia's death brings new disorder to his already troubled soul. An additional twist is his part in this new calamity. Although he cannot be completely sure of the reasons for Ophelia's death, his sense of guilt is not far below the surface. His rejection of her must be involved. Hence perhaps his overly dramatic proclamations of love before Laertes. Maybe, like the Queen-player, he 'doth protest too much', the wild clamour of one who knows he has sinned again by his neglect of a loved one. Certainly we see again the hot-headed side of Hamlet who loses all reason when he believes that someone has wronged him. The moment when Hamlet and Laertes struggle in the grave is one of terrible pain.

The scene is also significant for the way in which it binds Laertes more securely to the side of Claudius. The clash in the grave was an opportunity as well as a moment of crisis. Because Hamlet is so blindly self-righteous in his proclamations of love, and so oblivious to the pain of Laertes, the opportunity is lost. Laertes will persist in his ignoble plan to destroy his father's destroyer.

Scene 2

Hamlet's journey

Hamlet is telling Horatio about his sea voyage. He opened the letters of instruction which he was to convey to England, to find therein the request that he be beheaded. He forged a new letter ensuring that its bearers, Rosencrantz and Guildenstern, be put to death in his place.

Hamlet argues that Claudius deserves the fate which is about to befall him. Not only has he killed the former king, and 'whor'd' his mother, he has also 'Popp'd in between the election' and Hamlet's hopes for an orderly succession. It is now perfectly reasonable to **'quit him with arms'**, and rid the country of this **'canker of nature'**. As for Laertes, Hamlet regrets his impetuous behaviour at their last meeting (the graveside). He has come to recognise that in many ways their fates mirror each other. They have both lost a father, as well as Ophelia. It was simply his overpowering passion for Ophelia which overwhelmed Hamlet at the grave side. From now on he will 'court his favours'.

The challenge (duel)

At this point the courtier Osric enters. Osric announces that the king has wagered on a fencing duel between Hamlet and Laertes. Odds have been laid in Hamlet's favour. This matter can be immediately settled if Hamlet will enter the lists. Hamlet declares himself willing.

Horatio counsels against it

Horatio warns him that he will 'lose this wager' and suggests making excuses for Hamlet. But Hamlet will not be swayed from his course of action. Once more he refers to the heavenly disposition which will decide all such encounters, claiming that a **'special providence'** will decide his fate.

The duel

The king, the queen, Laertes, lords, Osric and attendants enter. The king invites the two combatants to join hands. Hamlet begs the pardon of Laertes for all that he has recently said and done. In his defence he pleads the 'madness' which has overtaken him of late. Seemingly reconciled, they move to pick up their foils. The king calls for 'stoups of wine' and proclaims that he will drink to Hamlet's success after 'the first or second hit'. For Hamlet is prepared a special cup into which the king will throw a 'union' (a pearl).

Gertrude poisoned

The match begins. The king drinks from his cup, inviting Hamlet to partake of his. Hamlet declines for the moment. He asks that it be set aside while he plays on. After the next bout Gertrude moves to wipe her son's brow, and drinks a toast to the good 'fortune' of Hamlet. In toasting Hamlet, she unwittingly drinks from the poisoned chalice. [Too late, Claudius forbids her to do so].

Hamlet and Laertes wounded

In the next scuffle Hamlet is wounded, but then the swords are accidentally swapped, and Hamlet wounds Laertes with his own sword. Both are thus afflicted by the poisoned tip meant only for

Hamlet. Laertes admits that he is **'justly kill'd with mine own treachery'**.

Laertes confesses

As the queen swoons, Claudius claims that it is simply the sight of blood which has caused her to faint. The queen denies this and, in her final breath, confesses that it is the drink which has led to her death. Laertes confesses to the villainy behind it all. Both he and Hamlet are to die by the same poisoned rapier and it is the king who is to blame.

Hamlet kills Claudius

Enraged, Hamlet stabs Claudius, condemning him as an **'incestuous, murdering, damned Dane'**. He also forces some of the poisoned draught down the throat of Claudius, demanding that the murderous king 'follow my mother' into death. The king dies.

Laertes and Hamlet die

Laertes now begs the forgiveness of Hamlet. Neither are to blame for the deaths of their respective fathers. He too dies. Hamlet vows to follow him in death. He bids the **'wretched queen, adieu'** and begs his beloved friend, Horatio, to ensure that his story is truthfully told.

Far off can be heard the sound of marching and a shot. Osric explains that it is Fortinbras, greeting the English ambassador outside the gates of Elsinore. Hamlet's last wish, before he passes away, is that the crown pass to this young warrior. Horatio bids **'good night'** to his **'sweet prince'**, and prays that **'flights of angels'** sing him to his final rest.

Fortinbras arrives

Fortinbras and the English ambassador enter. Fortinbras asks how 'proud death' has 'so bloodily struck' at 'so many princes'. The ambassador announces the news from England ('that Rosencrantz and Guildenstern are now dead'). Horatio orders that 'these bodies/ High on a stage be placed to the view', while he, Horatio, will speak to the 'yet unknowing world' of all that has befallen this royal house.

Horatio to tell the tale

Fortinbras hastens to lay his claim to the royal title. All in good time, he is informed by Horatio. But while 'men's minds are wild' with speculation about this current affair, it is more fitting that Hamlet, like a soldier, be given proper burial rites and acknowledged for the great king he might have been. All exit, bearing the bodies of the slain. A fusillade can be heard offstage.

Commentary Let us recognise first the absolute self-assurance which seems to have come over Hamlet. He is now a man firm in purpose, sure of the direction he is taking. He may have long agonised over the identity of the ghost. He may have pondered the morality of regicide. But all that equivocation has been cast off in the face of indubitable evidence of Claudius' evil scheming. Hamlet has now turned ruthless. He is content to dispatch his former friends to a certain fate with no 'shriving time allow'd' (no opportunity for Christian repentance). Not only must Claudius pay for his crimes, so must all who have assisted him, no matter how small their contribution. He now sees the guiding hand of providence behind all that he does. He has come to believe that there is a **'divinity that shapes our ends/ Rough-hew them how we will'**. This is the dangerous self-confidence of the true believer. Even the presence in his purse of his father's signet which sealed the forged letter and gave it the stamp of authenticity, was 'heaven ordinant'.

The final scene is significant for the way in which contrasting notions of 'honour' and dishonour are again on display. We see the honour of Hamlet as, now freed of all metaphysical doubts, he fights to the death to restore the honour of his father's house. We see the treachery of Laertes who pronounces himself satisfied with Hamlet's apology, yet is still ready to take the poisoned rapier. We see the duplicitous Claudius masterminding the action, ready if Hamlet does not die by the sword to swiftly introduce the poisoned chalice. In this he is shown to be undone and the righteous Hamlet vindicated, at least in the choice of royal successor. Honour has finally triumphed, however bloodily. Hamlet has had his wishes fulfilled. Claudius, caught out in the grossest of crimes and, unlike Laertes, unrepentant, is finally gorged with the very medicine he had intended for Hamlet. He is truly 'damned' as the wine is forced through his lips. Hamlet has managed to preserve his honour (in avenging his father's death), while still transcending the moral problems of cold-blooded murder. The slaying of Claudius is not a cruel premeditated act, but achieved in the heat of battle. Claudius comes to an ignoble end, as do Gertrude and the co-plotter, Laertes. Their royal line is terminated. Thus is honour preserved.

In his refusal to engage in direct planning throughout the play, Hamlet is finally vindicated. The providence that shapes all our ends can even encompass acts which appear rash and foolhardy. The vacillating, ineffectual Hamlet is revealed in the end as the 'noble' Hamlet, he that refused to act brutally until left no choice. The 'sweet prince' who was so uncomfortable in this world of 'flesh' and all the weaknesses to which it is heir, is delivered from that world. He now properly belongs in a kind of saintly sphere, preserved in all our memories. And who better to preserve and proclaim those memories than that most stoic defender of the truth, loyal Horatio.

Notes on Characters

Hamlet

Hamlet is probably the most famous of Shakespeare's tragedies, and certainly the most discussed. Not surprisingly, the debate, which has raged for centuries, focuses on the title character. Much has been made of Hamlet's famous indecision. What does it mean? Why does he find it impossible to act?

Hamlet the intellectual

The earliest and possibly still the most famous theory is most clearly associated with Samuel Taylor Coleridge, who pinpointed Hamlet's problem as one of too much 'intellectual activity, and the consequent proportionate aversion to real action.' (from *Shakespearean Criticism*) In other words, there are men of action, and intellectuals. Hamlet belongs to the latter category. Hamlet is a university student, a thinker, a philosopher. The theory does indeed find ready evidence. There is for instance the preponderance in the play of questions.

> Quote
>
> 'What art thou...?....What a piece of work is a man...and yet to me what is this quintessence of dust?....To be, or not to be, that is the question....'

Hamlet's confusion

Hamlet's speech is full of riddles, like his famous absurd interchanges with Polonius. The play abounds with contradictions, as Hamlet compares the different options available to him, the different possible 'truths'. There is lastly the evident self-bafflement of a man who does not even understand himself.

> Quote
>
> I do not know
> Why yet I live to say "This thing's to do," Sith I have
> cause, and will, and strength, and means
> To do't.

Whatever the truth of Coleridge's famous view of Hamlet as a man of thought rather than action, it was never wholly accepted, and by the early twentieth century, had been overshadowed by other psychological interpretations. The most famous of these is the idea of the Oedipus Complex, and it is associated with the Freudian analyst Ernest Jones (see Critical notes below). Jones claimed that Freud's theories perfectly fitted the profile of

The Freudian interpretation

> **Quote**
>
> a man who wants to murder his uncle-father, to be cruel to his mother, to abuse his girl-friend; and all this emerges in hysteria and sex-disgust....[In the Freudian interpretation] Claudius becomes identified as the figure who has acted both Hamlet's repressed desires: killed his father and slept with his mother....[So] the result is an intolerable strain which leads to paralysis of the will, hysterical self-disgust, sex-disgust, uncontrollable outbursts. (Nicholas Brooke, *Shakespeare's Early Tragedies*, Methuen, 1968)

The trouble with this view is that is really says more about the theoretical enthusiasms of the critic than it does about the character in the play. It completely ignores the moral concerns raised by Shakespeare, and treats a complex Elizabethan poetic drama as if it were a case study.

Hamlet's moral quandary

A safer view, and the one proposed by this commentary, is that Hamlet, if nothing else, was a man caught between conflicting moral imperatives. Being an 'thinker' may have slowed his urge to act. But the key problem for him was *what* to do. Certainly he had a duty to avenge his father (assuming the ghost was telling the truth). The whole thrust of revenge tragedies was to set up a character who was forced into a personal war against those who had committed appalling crimes, and vengeance was considered a reasonable course of action. But killing Claudius meant *murder*, the *slaughter of kin*, and worst, *regicide* (treasonable slaughter of a king), none at all acceptable from a Christian point of view. Should he just take his own life, to escape the dilemma, and end his misery? No, even that was forbidden by moral law. The Christian references in the play – the ghost's references to Purgatory, the king at prayer, Hamlet talking about the dogma on suicide, Ophelia's burial – are unavoidable, and cannot be discounted. Even when he was *sure* about Claudius, he couldn't act. So letting Claudius go was intolerable, but killing him was morally repugnant. The impasse was only broken when all was lost. Gertrude was dead, Hamlet himself was dying, and nothing mattered any more. As one critic has perceptively noted.

> How aware was Shakespeare of this moral muddle at the core of his play? And how aware was Hamlet that his behaviour as revenger and his beliefs as Christian were scarcely compatible? We shall never be able to answer these questions; but it is a fact that in the Renaissance the Christian ethic which says: 'Vengeance is mine, saith the Lord; I will repay' and the ethic of personal revenge co-existed side by side not merely as ways in which men actually behaved but as accepted, one might almost say respectable, moralities....and Hamlet himself, morally divided so perfectly that he does not seem aware of the division, may have seemed to many young men of the early 1600s a remarkably penetrating analysis of a young man like themselves. (Patrick Cruttwell, 'The Morality of Hamlet', in J. Jump, (ed). *Shakespeare's Hamlet*, Macmillan, 1968)

Like all other interpretations of the character, this one can only be offered as a possible view of what is a complex, and at times, contradictory text. But it does seem a piece with Shakespeare's other tragic heroes, Lear, Macbeth, Othello, whose problems are ultimately moral ones.

Hamlet the 'poet'   Likewise, the way an individual reader sees Hamlet as a person depends very much on what such a reader brings to the text. He has been read in a wide range of emotional colourings. At one end we have the highly sympathetic, if not romantic view of A.C. Bradley, who talked of Hamlet's 'exquisite sensibility' and asserted that

> He had the soul of the youthful poet...an unbounded delight and faith in everything good and beautiful. (*Shakespearean Tragedy*, Macmillan, 1904)

At the other extreme are versions of the character which assert his role as a revenger, a man of blood, however given to vacillation.

Hamlet:
all things
to all people

As Jan Kott observed, the play, by its very ambiguousness, is 'like a sponge' that sucks up whatever issues or concerns a particular age cares to bring to it. The same can probably be said for the title character. Is he a modern neurotic, a romantic 'sweet Prince', a moralising philosopher, a Christian, a revenger, or what? That is why, four centuries after Shakespeare gave him breath, he continues to perplex and divide us.

Claudius

In Claudius, too, we see conflicting qualities. The superficial Claudius is the villain of the revenge play – wily, unscrupulous, lying, prepared to do whatever it takes to preserve his power. For most of the play, we see Claudius effectively through Hamlet's eyes, as the usurper, the man who has claimed a throne which was never rightfully his. He also stands condemned by Hamlet for sharing the same kind of gross carnal appetites as Gertrude (wining and dining nightly, to the the puritanical Hamlet's disgust). However, we should not forget that these are the bitter tones of the outsider, of the one condemned to wait for a throne which should rightfully have passed to him.

Claudius
the villain

Redeeming
qualities

Yet there is another side to Claudius that we cannot completely ignore. In the prayer scene of Act 3, Scene 3, we perceive a genuine remorse in a man who has otherwise seemed nothing better than an odious schemer. There is no reason to doubt the sincerity of the man as he kneels before his God, and seeks forgiveness. He knows that his 'offense is rank', and that it 'smells to heaven'. Moreover, ever the realist, he admits that he cannot hope for the peace of forgiveness, while still enjoying the fruits of his ill-gotten gains. To give up the kingdom and the woman he loves in atonement for his crime is more than he can bear. Thus he is caught on the horns of his own dilemma. We may not admire him for his past course of action, but at least he does not go in for self-deception.

He also seems genuinely solicitous of Gertrude's welfare and there is a tenderness between them that cannot be completely written off as the residue of lust. After the death of Polonius he has more than enough evidence of Hamlet's ill-will towards him to have him put away permanently. Yet he cannot punish Hamlet without also punishing his mother who obviously adores her son ('The queen his mother/Lives almost by his looks'). And she is 'so conjunctive' to his 'life and soul' that he cannot imagine life without her. Although we know that he is planning to send him to England and to an almost certain death, there is at least some concern for Gertrude's welfare in all this.

Vicious qualities

Lest we begin to sentimentalise the man, we should also recall that he has only just spoken to his advisers about how Hamlet is 'loved of the distracted multitude' and how this prevents Claudius from putting 'the strong law on him'. In other words, there is a perfect concordance between his sentimental regard for Gertrude's welfare and his astute reading of the political wind. He is never less than a master 'politician'.

The justice of his end

And fittingly, his end is the result of one of his own schemes. His hastily-conceived plan to use Laertes as his pawn backfires horribly. The swords are exchanged in the duel, and the poisoned chalice drunk by Gertrude. His own death, at the hands of the young man he had thought first to control and then eliminate, follows swiftly.

In the final analysis Claudius is an archetypal villain, for all his human weaknesses. He wanted the throne and the queen, and he broke the moral law to take them. The misfortune signalled in the very first scene finally enfolds him and all those closest to him. Not only does justice catch up with him, but he *knows* it. He has condemned himself out of his own mouth in the prayer scene when he admits that he is not prepared to pay heaven's price and give up his ill-gotten gains. For this *hubris*, and for the terrible crimes of fratricide and regicide, he will pay the ultimate price – not just death (the loss of all he so prized), but everlasting damnation. The irony of Hamlet sparing him at confession is finally brought home to us. Claudius has, indeed, met his maker 'unshriv'd'.

Gertrude

A simple sensualist who follows her inclinations, not intending to do wrong, but seemingly unaware of the evil with which she is surrounded. That is a compelling way to read Gertrude.

How guilty is she?

In Shakespeare's version of the story, there is certainly *some* evidence of an adulterous affair with Claudius before the murder of old Hamlet. The ghost refers to Claudius as 'that adulterate beast', who has 'won to his shameful lust/The will of my most seeming-virtuous queen' (Act 1, Scene 5). Taken with the rest of his story (which seems to be borne out), it would appear that the affair began before the death of Hamlet's father. But of her unprincipled lust we have only Hamlet's wild ravings to rely upon. Of the unseemly haste with which she and Claudius have married there is little doubt, but the vision of her 'stew'd in corruption' springs mainly from Hamlet's fevered imagination. Certainly she appears to be innocent of any part in her husband's untimely death. How else can we read her reaction to 'The Mousetrap'? She seems more annoyed that Hamlet has 'offended' his father than perturbed by its hidden meaning. A meaning that would surely be obvious to any guilty party!

Gertrude's weakness

Perhaps Gertrude's chief weakness is that she is easily led. She allows Polonius to hide in her room before that crucial and ultimately murderous confrontation with Hamlet. She then allows herself to be browbeaten by a frenzied Hamlet as he rails against her seeming iniquities. After the death of Polonius and a thorough tongue lashing from Hamlet, she simply asks what she should do next. He instructs her to keep up appearances with Claudius and keep in mind that he, Hamlet, is not so much mad as crafty! No sooner is he out of earshot than she once more attaches herself to Claudius.

Good qualities

In her dealings with Ophelia she seems to show a genuine warmth and affection. At Ophelia's graveside she confesses that she had hoped that Ophelia could have become 'my Hamlet's wife'. Earlier she wondered if it was the loss of Ophelia's 'good beauties' which led to Hamlet's unsettled state. Yet she is also realistic enough to concede that it is more than likely her 'o'erhasty marriage' to Claudius which occasioned such grief.

Gertrude would appear to be as much a pawn in other people's schemes as she is a strong character in her own right. We have cause to blame her, cause to excuse her. Her death, finally, seems not so much a punishment of any inherent wickedness as an 'accident', another grim consequence of other, far more evil forces at work in the play.

Ophelia

Ophelia the victim

Ophelia can be seen as the simple victim. Thwarted by her father, abandoned by her lover, cast into profound grief by sudden bereavement, exacerbated by that abandonment, she goes mad and drowns herself. What else is there to say of her? She is yet another victim of the tragedy that sweeps through the world of this play.

Can we blame her for Hamlet's disdain? Does she give in to Polonius too easily? It is difficult to sustain such arguments, given what we know of the role of women, especially young unmarried women, in those times. How could she do anything but obey, and play the part allocated her?

We must keep in mind that for a girl of Ophelia's class there would have been a great emphasis on filial piety in her upbringing. Furthermore, she seems to be a victim of *two* powerful patriarchs within her family: Polonius with his devious and hastily-conceived plans for her advancement, and Laertes with his hypocritical diatribes against the lusts of Hamlet. She certainly seems singularly ill-advised in these matters, as we have little evidence of Hamlet the wastrel, and much to suggest that he is an exceedingly high-minded and principled suitor.

While allowing herself to be used in the plans by Polonius and Claudius to root out the source of Hamlet's disquiet, it would be churlish to point the finger of blame at Ophelia. She seems to be completely under her father's spell and, in fact, plays her assigned role very poorly. Clearly she is out of her depth, especially when seeking to handle an increasingly angry and irrational Hamlet.

Ophelia and 'lost love' of the story

What is perhaps most interesting about Ophelia is how she represents the tragedy of lost love. At first, there is a defensive coquetry about her dealings with the prince, but a simmering passion between her and Hamlet breaks through, ironically, when all hope of love is gone. In the sexual banter between them before the dumbshow begins, we gain a glimpse of a more sensual side to her nature. Matching Hamlet's bawdy jests with lewd remarks about 'country' girls, and how it will cost her a 'groaning' if she is to take the edge off his sexual appetite, she appears almost light-hearted. There is ample evidence that she loves Hamlet, as the poignant and beautiful speech 'O what a noble mind is here o'erthrown!' makes clear. And following the death of her father, at the hands of her would-be husband, when she loses her reason (unlike Hamlet it is *real* madness), she appears bedecked in flowers and singing snatches of songs, many of which testify to love. 'Before you tumbled me/ You promised me to wed', she croons, a pathetic parody of a love which was never fulfilled.

Ophelia seems sensitive, gentle and loving. Hamlet, we deduce,

Why Ophelia went mad

must have once been an attentive suitor. She certainly has found no fault with him. But the machinations of Polonius, and Hamlet's twisted vision of all women as 'fallen' (after the death of his father and the precipitate, 'incestuous' remarriage of his mother) conspire to wreck any chances of their love being consummated. She is left with what she incorrectly sees as a 'noble mind…'o'erthrown', Hamlet's insanity, when it is really the wreck of their relationship. That, together with her father's death, will rapidly lead to her insanity. An even deeper irony is that she is reunited with Hamlet by death, as the grave scene brings him back to a realisation of what he lost in her.

Ophelia is a victim. Feminists have written passionately about her, seeing her as destroyed by patriarchal, anti-female attitudes. Romantics have seen her as a maiden with a broken heart. As perhaps the only really 'innocent' character caught up in the tragedy, she prompts our sympathy more than all the others. Of the many horrors in Hamlet, the madness and despair of Ophelia is probably the most affecting.

Polonius

A satire on the obsequious courtier, a figure of comic relief – that is how most people have seen Polonius. In taking such an easy road to interpretation, however, they overlook the more sinister aspects of his character.

Polonius the politician

Polonius is the original master of political intrigue. One does not make it to court and then ascend the greasy pole of political influence without hurting many people along the way. He is no exception. All considerations, familial and personal, must be suborned to the primary aim of retaining the ear of the king. There is no more telling example of this than his cruelty to Ophelia.

Polonius the bullying patriarch

This cruelty is evidenced in our first encounter with the pair after Polonius has farewelled Laertes on his departure for France. (Act 1, Scene 3). He completely ignores Ophelia's protestations that Hamlet has been never less than honourable in his dealings with her. He is quite inconsistent in the advice he offers. First he urges her to play hard to get, thus upping the ante in the matrimonial stakes. Then he orders her to cut off all contact with Hamlet. Herein are sown the seeds for the tragedy to follow. Hamlet completely misinterprets Ophelia's coldness towards him and never recovers his original vision of her loveliness. In his mind he becomes another painted whore out to beguile and trick all men.

This would be bad enough, but the later actions of Polonius are unforgivable. Betraying no sensitivity to the plight of his daughter, Polonius now drags her before Claudius to confess that the courtship was abandoned on his instructions. He even reads the contents of a letter which Hamlet has written to Ophelia in her presence. Knowing that he is on slippery ice, he vows that all this is the source of Hamlet's madness and that it was only Ophelia's lowly station in life that led him, Polonius, to issue the instructions in the first place.

What a craven performance this is! We can only surmise that the original instructions to his daughter were designed to remove her from contact with one who was 'contaminated' in the eyes of the court. All the homely wisdom about lustful men is but a smokescreen. Having to his horror discovered that he might have been the cause of Hamlet's madness, he now desperately seeks to cover his tracks by giving yet another weak excuse for his actions. It was all to ensure that Hamlet married someone more fitted to his station in life! Even this sycophantic performance is later undermined by Gertrude's statement that she saw it as a most fitting match.

His final disgraceful act is to 'loose' Hamlet on his daughter so that he and Claudius may spy upon them and glean Hamlet's intent. There is an unconscionable coarseness in all this that Hamlet appears to easily perceive. Indeed his aspersions at the expense of Ophelia could partly reflect the prostituted role into which Polonius has forced her. She has become a mere pawn in the power politics of the court and can be readily sacrificed to its needs.

In all this we perceive the most despicable of men flattering and gaining favour with the king. No doubt they are bound together in an alliance of mutual need and satisfaction. Polonius has helped smooth the path to accession for the new king. 'The head is not more native to the heart ….. Than is the throne of Denmark to thy father', Claudius tells Laertes in the first act. The new king owes him that favour at least, and seems prepared to overlook the lapses in judgement that make him such an unreliable adviser. At the same time Polonius must continue to court the king's favour if his addled wits are not to cost him more than his job!

It is easy to dismiss Polonius as some kind of senile old fool, but he is much more than that. One did not arrive at that position in court without having been an astute judge of matters of state, and Claudius acknowledges as much. Despite his errors of judgement he is still a force to be reckoned with. Although his crimes do not begin to match those of Claudius, he is similarly obsessed with, and corrupted by power and pride. His death is a test of how we feel about him. While we no doubt experience the horror of knowing what a costly mistake it will be for Hamlet, we are unlikely to feel much grief. Here was a man who pretended to be high-principled, but was in reality a devious manipulator, and he dies, ironically but fitly, caught in one of his own schemes.

Laertes

Laertes the man of action

If Hamlet is contemplative man, then Laertes is action man. His anger at finding his father slain gives rise to the need for immediate vengeance, stayed only by Claudius' plan of a rigged sword fight. Although that fight does not turn out as intended, Laertes' death by the sword is a natural extension of his character. Like a more educated Fortinbras, he makes decisions, and then acts as he thinks best.

Good qualities

In some ways he is a sympathetic character. His love for Ophelia and Polonius ring true. His concern to 'square' things with Hamlet at the end is a tribute to his sense of honour. In a sense, he is another good man brought down by the tragedy.

Less admirable qualities

Less admirable perhaps is the rather patronising advice he is inclined to dish out to his sister. Clearly he is fond of her, but his words of wisdom about avoiding men and their wiles has unpleasant echoes of his father's hypocritical sermonising. Her rebuff to Laertes about his playing the libertine, while treading 'the primrose path of dalliance' is well earned.

Also deserving of our condemnation is the unworthy alliance he makes with Claudius. Full of dudgeon upon his return to Denmark, outraged at the death of his father, and grief stricken at the loss of his sister, we can easily sympathise with his plight. Yet so quickly does he switch his allegiance once Claudius informs him of the cause of Polonius' death! For a man of honour he is remarkably ready to improve upon Claudius' plan for a sharpened duelling sword with his own nasty variation (poison).

Redemption in the end

Only in the dying moments of his duel with Hamlet does Laertes regain his dignity as a man of honour and bring their quarrel to a fitting end. Admitting that his ill-conceived plan hatched with Claudius is 'almost against my conscience', he seems to virtually 'throw' the fight, allowing Hamlet an easy victory at the end. In this moment of reconciliation with Hamlet ('I am justly killed with mine own treachery') Laertes can 'exchange forgiveness' with his old foe, as both have lost a father and both are about to lose their lives.

Horatio

Because he is part Chorus (to Hamlet's misfortune), and part foil (to Hamlet's very different personality), we tend to overlook Horatio. Yet he may represent a philosophical option. The stoic who keeps his counsel, endures whatever the world brings, and lives to tell the tale. Can we read him as the sort of man Hamlet should have been? The man 'whose blood and judgement are so well commingled' offers the kind of wise counsel Hamlet needs at times of crisis.

Horatio – the only honest man in the play

Certainly he is the only man in whom Hamlet places an absolute trust. Horatio is the one man who has returned to Elsinore from Wittenberg to be present at the funeral of Hamlet's father. His presence was not commanded and, unlike so many others, he appears to owe the new king no favours. He is the man who stands beside Hamlet and urges reason when the ghostly apparition threatens to unsettle Hamlet's mind. It is as though Hamlet recognises, at some unconscious level, that Horatio complements him in the areas in which he is defective. Where he can be rash and impulsive, Horatio is calm and considered. Where Hamlet is given to extraordinary flights of fancy, Horatio is firmly grounded in the need for evidence. What can we know through our senses, asks this philosopher. Don't talk to me about ghosts until I have heard them and seen them with my own eyes. Hamlet may chide him for not conceding that 'there are more things in heaven and earth' than dreamt of in his (realist) philosophy, but he recognises that this man is not 'passion's slave'. In tones of great passion he swears that 'I will wear him/ In my heart's core' as one worthy of an infinite trust.

Most telling of all, it is Horatio to whom he turns in his dying moments. This man, given to little hyperbole and no falsehood, is the one best suited to draw his 'breath in pain' in order to tell Hamlet's fatal story.

Notes on Themes and Issues

Appearance and reality, seeming and substance

Quote

Seems, madam? Nay, it is. I know not 'seems'.

So much of the play is taken up with this antithesis, so deeply embedded is it in the very structure of the play, that it is perhaps easily overlooked. Nonetheless we must be alert to this fundamental dislocation.

What Hamlet sees – decadence and dissembling

Beneath the seeming calm and dignity of the court lie festering secrets. The appearance of respectability and normality, is, it turns out, an illusion. Hamlet's great first soliloquy is all about his despair at the truth, the 'rotten' things below the surface.

Quote

How weary, stale, flat, and unprofitable
Seem to me all the uses of this world!

Gertrude

The immediate cause of his despair is his mother's hasty and 'incestuous' marriage to Claudius. Could Gertrude's displays of affection for her late husband be anything other than mere show, if they can so readily be put aside? Hamlet himself seems very sure that the 'wicked speed' and 'dexterity' with which she buried the old king betokens scant affection. What then is he to make of her protestations of love and concern for himself? There can be no more radical undermining of one's confidence in the world's order than the realisation that the foundations of family life are shaky.

Claudius

Worse is to come, as Hamlet learns that his uncle is not just a wily rogue and a 'satyr', but a murderer as well. The king's seeming piety disguises those abominable crimes fraticide and regicide.

Ophelia

Meanwhile the prince looks at his one-time beloved, Ophelia, and finds her calculating and cold. Is she playing female games too

Hamlet

like his mother? Is the ghost telling the truth, or deceiving him? Can her father be trusted, or is he a liar too? Are his old friends Rosencrantz and Guildenstern in league with him, or the stooges of the king? Most agonising of all perhaps, is Hamlet's self-perception. Is he the noble man he thinks, or a cowardly fool? His famous indecision begins to look not so much like dilly-dallying as sheer perplexity. What is real? What is pretence? The mimicry of the play-within-the-play imitates the mimicry (of goodness) and duplicity that seems to surround Hamlet. When Hamlet utters the famous line

> There are more things in heaven and earth, Horatio,
> Than are dreamt of in your philosophy.

it refers primarily to the ghost. But it could be taken as a more general text, in line with

> There is nothing either good or bad but thinking makes it so.

Philosophy is celebrated, sometimes satirised, for questioning what appear to be obvious realities. How do we know? What is truth? Psychology explores similar territory. If people play roles, as they must, what are they *really* like? How reliable a guide are words or actions to the truth of a person's being?

The world's a 'stage'

This theme is the very key to understanding *Hamlet*. Many of the other problems which seem to bedevil any study of the play fall into place once its ramifications have been realised. For the dreadful realisation that the whole world is a 'stage' prompts three consequences, all equally unpalatable for this profoundly ethical man.

Hamlet must pretend too

The first is that Hamlet still must make his way in this world full of scheming. He must don a mask, play a part, lie and deceive *too*. The world is a very slippery, dangerous place in which no-one can be trusted. Even the companions of his boyhood, Rosencrantz and Guildenstern, are not to be taken at face value. They are on a mission from the king to help discover the cause of Hamlet's madness. They may have an even more sinister mission. He is not to know, and they are not to be trusted.

Hamlet's self-doubt

The second impact is on his self-belief. Can we trust ourselves when we say something or feel anything? Or are we also playing tricks upon our own psyche? Engaging in self-deception? So often Hamlet seems to doubt the authenticity of his own emotional states, so radically shaken is his confidence in the moral order. This self-doubt peaks during the soliloquy in Act 2, Scene 2, where he laments his own inaction and contrasts it unfavourably with the ability of a player to 'act' a part. The actor can work himself up into a profound state of grief for Hecuba

Quote

For Hecuba! What's Hecuba to him or he to Hecuba That he should weep for her?'

How would the actor behave if he *really* had something to weep over, ponders Hamlet. Why, he would 'drown the stage with tears'!

Hamlet's despair

The last and most subtle consequence is how the loss of certainty produces a kind of despair. The world becomes a 'weary, stale, flat and unprofitable' place when the realisation of how flawed and unknowable we all are begins to dawn on the mind. It is as if Hamlet has been given a giant puzzle, and has tried as hard as he can to solve it, only to discover that there is no solution! We will never know. We will go on playing games, and never knowing about other people, until the tragedy is ended. This sort of world-weary disgust creates a kind of existential *angst* in Hamlet that would not be out of place in any play written this century.

Hamlet the philosopher

Hamlet is, by inclination as well as training, a *philosopher*, and one of his preoccupations throughout the play is a traditional concern of philosophy. What is *real*? How do we *know* what to believe? From the ghost's claim to be his dead father (in Act One), which turns out to be true, to the apparent assurances he has of a fair fight (in Act Five), which turn out to be false, we are repeatedly confronted with this issue. Hamlet's famous uncertainty is largely the problem of a thoughtful man contemplating life, and finding it frighteningly ambiguous. Perhaps the clearest metaphor for this theme is 'the-play-within-the-play'. Is everything an act? Are all just playing parts? What is the truth? Can we ever be sure?

Revenge and honour or moral purity?

Hamlet's ethical quandary

Quote

> Now might I do it pat, now 'a is a-praying,
> And now I'll do't. And so 'a goes to heaven,
> And so I am revenged. That would be scanned
> [re-examined].
> A villain kills my father, and for that
> I, his sole son, do this same villain send
> To heaven.

Hamlet's rationalising is brilliant. He will not kill Claudius when the moment presents itself, because that would be a debased revenge (sending him to heaven and not to hell). Or is the truth otherwise? Can he stab a man in the back, while he is praying, a man who happens to be his uncle and his king? Hamlet constantly berates himself about his inaction, but there remains an invisible barrier to the murder he feels he has to commit.

Hamlet must kill for honour

Deep below this is an ethical dilemma: the call to knightly 'honour' on one hand, and the call to be a Christian 'gentleman' on the other. We think of the warrior Fortinbras and his readiness to take revenge on Denmark for the slight inflicted upon his father by Hamlet's father. Hamlet is faced with much more than a mere slight to his family honour. If he is correct in his suspicions, murder has been committed. Yet how can he act when the call to action is also a call to regicide (killing a king)? How can he so act when much of his information is gleaned from a ghost who may be a manifestation of demonic powers, beckoning him to his soul's destruction?

Hamlet must not kill as a Christian

Furthermore, he is deeply enmeshed in the paradox of what it was to be a Christian and also a 'gentleman'. The warrior code, which calls for decisive, even bloody action, is at odds with the precepts of Christianity, which call for goodness, saintliness. The Christian code calls on one to turn the other cheek, to forgive one's enemies. It values goodness above greatness, meekness above strength. Indeed the very call to 'greatness' in the honour code (the greatness of a warrior) was an invitation to mortal sin (committing murder, and 'self-slaughter' when all else failed), according to the dictates of the Church.

Hamlet is a victim of this paradox and only late in the play does he resolve it. The circuit-breakers are two – self defence and the need to right another wrong. In Act 5, Scene 2, he explains to Horatio how he can now see his way clear. All doubts about the manner of his father's death are laid to rest. The despicable actions of his mother are temporarily forgotten. Even the political trickery of Claudius is of lesser importance. For what he now has is incontrovertible evidence of Claudius' plan for his (Hamlet's) *own* destruction. The sealed letters to the English court permit of no other interpretation. Thus, very late in the piece, *does* Hamlet resolve the paradox of the Christian who would also be a gentleman. Heaven itself calls for justice, for revenge upon this man who would slay the rightful heir to the throne of Denmark.

Hamlet's moral dilemma is central to the play. In confronting the call to revenge, he also at least partly subverts it. As George Bernard Shaw so perceptively wrote:

Quote

In the soliloquy beginning 'O, what a rogue and peasant slave am I' Shakespeare described this moral bewilderment....What happened to Hamlet was what had happened fifteen hundred years before to Jesus. Born into the vindictive morality of Moses he has evolved into the Christian perception of the futility and wickedness of revenge and punishment, founded on the simple fact that two blacks do not make a white. But he is not philosopher enough to comprehend this as well as apprehend it. When he finds he cannot kill in cold blood he can only ask 'Am I a coward?' When he cannot nerve himself to recover his throne he can account for it only by saying 'I lack ambition'. Had Shakespeare plumbed his play to the bottom [of this moral argument] he would hardly have allowed Hamlet to send Rosencrantz and Guildenstern to their death by a forged death warrant without a moment's scruple.
(G.B.Shaw, Postscript to *Back to Methuselah*, 1945)

While much critical comment has been devoted over the years to why Hamlet couldn't act, deep down it can be read as a moral quandary. To right a wrong with another wrong is problematic and the philosopher in Hamlet rebels against it. Only when forced, almost against his will, into the role of warrior, and knowing he is dying, does he break out of inaction and take the revenge he has too long, and perhaps, too properly, postponed.

The problem of Hamlet's 'madness'

Quote

How strange or odd some'er I bear myself
(As I perchance hereafter shall think meet
To put an antic disposition on), [never show]
That you know aught of me [my strategy].

O what a noble mind is here o'erthrown.

Evidence his 'madness' is feigned

An extraordinary amount of time and critical attention has been devoted to this vexed problem. Yet we have clear evidence in Hamlet's own self-assessment (Act 2, Scene 2). Here he reassures his old friends that he is but 'mad north-north west'. When the wind is southerly he knows 'a hawk from a handsaw'. In other words, he is perfectly aware of the effect that his 'madness' is having upon those around him. The only thing that is odd about this confession is that it should be made to these two whom he has started to suspect are part of the 'plot' against him.

This assumed 'madness' is a necessary part of the cloak or disguise with which he has surrounded himself. He lives in a kingdom where nothing is as it seems. He lives in a palace where treachery is to be found everywhere and where even old friends have been conscripted to the traitor's cause. Perhaps Hamlet would nowadays be derided as 'paranoid'. But as the modern saying would have it: just because he is paranoid, it doesn't mean that they are not out to get him!

Nor can we overlook the simple fact that early in the play he tells Marcellus and Horatio – the latter being the only man he trusts completely – that he will 'put an antic disposition on'. This admission comes immediately after the weird confrontation with the ghost who seems to be scurrying around underneath the floorboards of the stage. Moreover, the 'disguise' of madness is a very effective ploy. Even if his motives are hard to understand, it places extraordinary pressure on young Ophelia when he appears before her 'with a look so piteous in purport/ As if he had been loosed out of hell'. His 'antic disposition' before the hapless Polonius unsettles *him* on more than one occasion. The role of madman has the effect of wrongfooting his opponents. It certainly places Claudius on his guard and precipitates the series of events which eventually unmasks the villain.

Signs of mental instability

Having said all that, there are other elements to Hamlet's behaviour not so readily explained. There is his almost manic disposition around Ophelia. The silent treatment meted out to her (in the scene already alluded to), betokens a mind at the very edge. What can be gained by the extraordinary silent treatment of Ophelia at this point? Or the mocking cruelty he deals out to her after the 'accidental' meeting in Act 3, Scene 1? The crass sexual jokes, the ordering of her to a 'nunnery'? This seems more than the pique of the spurned lover. Ophelia is certainly convinced at this point that 'a noble mind is here o'erthrown'. We can only speculate that if not temporarily insane, he is certainly *maddened* by yet another example of the treachery with which he is surrounded. We must favour the latter interpretation. It is the only one which dovetails with his obsessions with 'frail' women. At other times his behaviour is frenzied and irrational. It bespeaks a mind at the end of its tether – a man driven beyond all endurance, an exhaustion partly of his own making. For so long has he stewed over his inaction, for so long has he been paralysed by doubt, plagued by fear of wrongdoing, that the pressure tells on him. Hence the wild, hysterical changes in mood at once brisk and matter-of-fact (dealing with the players and Rosencrantz and Guildenstern), then downcast and almost suicidally melancholy.

Hamlet's problems

Hamlet suffers wild mood swings (bi-polar affective disorder?), is cast down into the slough of despondency (depression?), appears to see enemies everywhere (paranoid delusion?), and is certainly fixated on the mother figure in a way that has delighted thousands of Freudians. A simpler explanation is offered by his mother: he is 'Mad as the sea and wind, when both contend'. In other words, he is a man in the grip of terrible opposing forces which threaten to tear him apart. He has failed to act at a time where a less introspective man (Fortinbras?), would have acted immediately and brutally. He is fatally hesitant in his desire to do the right thing, to save his own soul and yet see wrongs put right. That failure to act has bred in him a kind of self-disgust, a deep self-loathing, that manifests itself in wild affective mood swings. At one moment he is on top of affairs, making plans, and about to grasp the nettle. The next moment he is cast down, unsure of his ability to carry through a plan of action. *Hamlet is a man eminently unsuited to action.* He is a thinker cast in the role of man of action. When all around him are playing their parts to perfection, he seems eminently uneasy in his role.

The battle of good and evil

Fie on't, ah, fie, 'tis and unweeded garden
That grows to seed. Things rank and gross in nature
 Possess it merely.

*Evil as a
key theme*

That something is rotten in the state of Denmark, indeed the whole world of *Hamlet*, cannot be mistaken. The play confronts us not only with a set of devious characters, lying, cheating and killing, but innumerable speeches about the corruption to which flesh is heir.

Like all tragedies, *Hamlet* is an account of human wretchedness, of lives destroyed and needless suffering. Indeed, one critic actually asserts that in this work:

the Tragic Hero, ultimately, is humanity itself; and what humanity is suffering from, in Hamlet is not a specific evil, but Evil itself. The murder is only the chief of many manifestations of it, the particular case which is the mainspring of the tragic action....Shakespeare's real theme is not the moral or theological or social problem of crime, still less its effect on a single mind and soul, but the corroding power of sin [which he represents] not as a single 'error of judgement' but as a hydra with many heads....In *Hamlet* [the corruption] spreads from soul to soul, as a contagion, as when Laertes is tempted by Claudius, or, most notably, when, by his mother's example and Polonius' based inspired interference, Hamlet's love is corrupted into lewdness, or when he turns against his two compromised friends and pitilessly sends them to death....Shakespeare saw [tragedy] as an evil quality which, once it has broken loose, will feed upon itself and on anything else that it can find until it reaches its natural end. (H.D.F.Kitto, 'Hamlet as Religious Drama', in the Jump anthology, cited above)

Redemption

Yet the portrait of life which the play offers is not completely black, and is certainly not an affirmation of immorality. Justice is finally done, even though Hamlet is lost along with the evil-doers. The moral order is finally restored, and Horatio's parting words to Hamlet give him his due as a noble man, a 'sweet Prince' whose tragedy was to be caught in bad times.

If the play had ended with the villain triumphant, we would rightly worry about what that argued. But the evil are punished. This is a tragedy, so the good suffer too. However, the ending brings us to a peace after sin and retribution, to a world made morally whole again.

Fortune, destiny, dissolution and death

> *Quote*
>
> Now get you to my lady's chamber, and tell her, let her paint an inch thick, to this favour [look, ie being just a skull] she must come.

Ophelia was wrong about Hamlet being mad, but right in her understanding that things had fallen apart for him. The play is full of a sense of paradise having been lost, of decline and the imminence of death.

*The 'darkness' in **Hamlet***

The most famous scene in *Hamlet*, known even to people who have never read the play, is the graveyard scene. 'Alas, poor Yorick...I knew him Horatio.' A skull, a dead jester, a mad girl who throws herself into the water and drowns, a murdered king, a poisoned cup, and the deaths at the end of all the main characters – these are what give *Hamlet* its notoriously dark flavour.

Tragedy is always couched in the specifics of a particular set of terrible actions, but its power to move us is more general. In the fatal misfortune of individuals, whose destiny singled them out for pain, in the sense of loss, horror and death, tragedy confronts us with the darkness of life. Hamlet has what feels like an almost

Melancholy world view of the play

modern sense of the meaninglessness of existence. When Hamlet speaks of shrinking from 'The undiscovered country, from whose bourn No traveller returns', he is expressing the ancient and familiar fear of mortality. Yet, looking around him he is filled with despair.

An unkind fate, a sense that things are breaking down around him, coupled with a fear of death: that is why Hamlet is the classic study in melancholy. The gloom of his vision, an Elizabethan reprise of the ancient Greeks' tragic view of man's condition, is very much part of what this play is about.

What the Critics Say

Hamlet is probably the most famous of Shakespeare's plays. It has always been admired, and has been produced almost without cessation since it was written almost four hundred years ago. Why is it so popular? Here is what one Victorian commentator explained as its fascination.

Quote

Hamlet, in spite of a prejudice current in certain circles that if now produced for the first time it would fail, is the most popular play in our language. It amuses thousands annually, and it stimulates the minds of millions. Performed in barns and minor theatres oftener than in Theatres Royal, it is always and everywhere attractive. The lowest and most ignorant audiences delight in it. The source of the delight is twofold: First, its reach of thought on topics is the most profound; for the dullest soul can feel grandeur which it cannot understand, and will listen with hushed awe to the out-pourings of a great meditative dramatic variety. Only consider for a moment the striking effects it has in the Ghost; the tyrant murderer; the terrible adulterous queen; the melancholy hero, doomed to so awful a fate; the poor Ophelia, broken-hearted and dying in madness; the play within a play, entrapping the conscience of the King; the ghastly mirth of the gravediggers; the funeral of Ophelia interrupted by a quarrel over her grave betwixt her brother and her lover; and, finally, the horrid bloody dénouement. Such are the figures woven in the tapestry by passion and poetry. Add thereto the absorbing fascination of profound thoughts.
(G.H.Lewes, *Life and Works of Goethe*, 1855)

Indeed, perhaps no other play in the history of English letters has attracted so much critical attention as *Hamlet*. Hamlet, the character, seems irresistibly fascinating to other literary figures,

Johnson

while its themes of jealousy, revenge, honour and madness seem as tirelessly perennial as when Samuel Johnson first speculated about them in 1765.

Johnson himself found fault with the play. He wondered whether there is offered to us sufficient motivation for Hamlet's feigned madness. Or is it too inconsistent in its presentation, too erratic in its unfolding to create that necessary consistency of characterisation so essential to great drama. In simpler terms, he asked, can we believe that this character is real? According to Johnson, Hamlet 'does nothing which he might not have done with the reputation of sanity'. The implication seems to be that there is a kind of histrionic excess to *Hamlet*. Johnson was also troubled by the bizarre cruelties of Hamlet. He felt that Hamlet treated Ophelia with 'wanton cruelty' and that Hamlet's cheerful efforts to damn the souls of Claudius, Rosencrantz and Guildenstern, were monstrous. On the other hand, Johnson also praised the play for its great 'variety' (complexity and range).

Knight

G. Wilson Knight in *The Wheel Of Fire* took up the same theme. For Knight, 'Hamlet is inhuman. He has seen through humanity. And this inhuman cynicism, however justifiable in this case, on the plane of causality and individual responsibility, is a deadly and venomous thing'. For Knight, Hamlet is a 'superman among men ….because he has walked and held converse with Death'. The principal theme of *Hamlet* 'is an element of evil in the state of Denmark'.

Goethe

For Johann Goethe, writing in 1796, the problem was one of Aristotelian tragedy (see introductory Genre notes). That is, Hamlet is a type of tragic hero, brought down by a fatal flaw in his character. That flaw was a failure of nerve. Hamlet's is a 'beautiful, pure, noble and most moral nature, without the strength of nerve which forms a hero'. He is an individual whose sheer intellect is too great to find the crudeness of action easy.

Coleridge

Samuel Taylor Coleridge echoes this notion of an overly intellectualising man, ill-suited to action. However he also points out the role of divinity in shaping our ends, something to which Hamlet himself alludes towards the end of the play. For Coleridge the 'due balance between the real and the imaginary world … does not exist'. Hence the hero suffers from 'great, enormous intellectual activity, and a consequent aversion to real action'.

Eliot

T.S. Eliot, a man much concerned with the integrity of art, sees the 'problem' of *Hamlet* as a failure of artistry. In his words, the play is 'almost certainly an artistic failure'. He felt that the suffering of Hamlet, the indecision and the disgust (particularly at his mother), seems improbably overdone. He is 'dominated by an emotion which is inexpressible, because it is in excess of the facts as they appear'. In other words, Shakespeare has created an unnecessarily complex figure, given to implausible emotions, which neither its creator nor the audience can understand.

Grebainer

Others take a completely contrary position, arguing that Hamlet is a perfectly composed and healthy figure. For Bernard Grebanier (*The Heart of Hamlet*), we should look not so much at what Hamlet says as what he does. If we examine his actions, according to Grebanier, we will find him 'not melancholy, not complex-ridden, not pessimistic, not even disillusioned basically – but a healthy, vigorous man, much in love with, who, given the slightest opportunity, is happy cheerful, companionable and kind'. For Grebanier, Hamlet fails 'not because he is too timid, too sensitive, too thoughtful, or too scrupulous, but because he is too rash, too overweening, too heedless'.

Bradley

Like Grebanier, A.C. Bradley, in his famous essay on *Shakespearean Tragedy*, sees Hamlet as a man much debilitated by melancholia. For Bradley, melancholy 'accounts for Hamlet's energy as well as his lassitude'. The man is 'by temperament .. inclined to nervous instability' and all it takes is the 'moral shock of the sudden ghastly disclosure of his mother's true nature' to unhinge him completely.

Freud

These early attempts at explaining away Hamlet's dilemma in terms of various neuroses reached its apogee with the teachings of Sigmund Freud. Indeed a 'psychoanalytical' reading of Hamlet and his actions came to dominate literary criticism in the early decades of this century. Inspired by the seminal work by Sigmund Freud (*The Interpretation of Dreams*), and led by his disciples such as Ernest Jones, such a reading places enormous emphasis on Hamlet's relationship with his mother.

This is an interpretation which requires us to subscribe to the psychoanalytical theory of the so-called Oedipus Complex, a neurotic state in which the adult has not outgrown the childhood fantasy that his mother belongs to him and that the father is an interloper. If one has not successfully negotiated this childhood phase of development, one is always and unconsciously in a struggle with the father figure whom one wishes to murder, but of whom is also afraid. According to Freud, Hamlet is 'able to do anything – except take vengeance on the man who did away with his father and took that father's place with his mother, the man who shows him the repressed wishes of his own childhood realised. Thus the loathing which should drive him on to revenge is replaced in him by self-reproaches, by scruples of conscience, which remind him that he himself is literally no better than the sinner whom he is about to punish'. For Freud, the 'distaste for sexuality expressed by Hamlet in his conversation with Ophelia fits in very well with this'.

Modern variations

What is interesting about all these interpretations is that they reflect to a great extent the pre-occupations of the various ages which produced them. The latter part of the nineteenth century saw doctors and other thinkers much taken up with issues of mental health. Reviving medieval notions of the 'humours', they speculated endlessly about melancholia and other psychic ills to which we humans are susceptible. It is easy to see those influences on Bradley. Similarly, the craze for Freud and Freudian explanations of human conduct were much in vogue in the early decades of this century and Ernest Jones was an enormously influential disciple of Freud's.

Feminists, predictably, have taken Shakespeare to task for his allegedly misogynistic protagonist – pointing out the scorn that Hamlet pours on Gertrude ('Frailty by name is woman') and Ophelia (' You jig and amble and you lisp...').

In all these readings, from the Aristotelian (*Hamlet* as a tragedy of character), the ethical (*Hamlet* as a tragedy of conflicting moral codes), through to the Existential (*Hamlet* as a play about the absurdity of life and the imminence of death) – there is some truth, no doubt. Like most great texts, this one reflects the dominant ideologies of each passing era. Interpretation is, as always, very much the prerogative of the individual reader.

Performance Interpretations of *Hamlet*

Hamlet has always been one of the most popular, if also most difficult, of Shakespeare's plays.

Since the title role is so attractive, and so enigmatic, lead actors tended to make it a 'star vehicle' in such a way as to advance their own status with the public. The same, interestingly, continues in modern film adaptations. David Garrick, in the eighteenth century, portrayed Hamlet as a noble prince, not as a dithering coward. He actually cut parts of the script that portrayed Hamlet in less than flattering light (the almost killing Claudius at prayer scene, the 'execution' of Rosencrantz and Guildenstern).

Nineteenth century productions likewise presented the prince as a heroic, Romantic figure, suffering from too much nobility of spirit to resolve his problems swiftly. The tendency in earlier centuries was for a fuller, 'historical' setting – with often expensive recreations of Elsinore castle.

In the twentieth century, criticism and performance took on a variety of forms. The traditional 'costume drama' approach, with lavish sets, spectacular costumes and 'realism', continued alongside bare stage modernist interpretations, and post-modern revisions, in which Hamlet might be in modern dress or relocated to some twentieth century context. Interpretations of the character have varied enormously – from the 'Romantic' to the 'mad.'

Film versions of Hamlet

There have in fact been some 50 different screen versions of this famous play. However, it is probably fair to say that the best known versions are these:

• The Olivier *Hamlet* (1948) – with Sir Laurence Olivier as Hamlet, this black and white 'classic' was for decades the definitive film version. Although long (155 minutes) and highly theatrical in style, it showed off the great actor to magnificent effect and was faithful to the original.
• The Nicol Williamson *Hamlet* (1969) – directed by Tony Richardson, and with the quirky Williamson as the prince, Anthony

Hopkins as Claudius and Marianne Faithful (the famous singer) as Ophelia, this film was a mixed success. At 117 minutes, it was not too long, but critics consider it somewhat 'stagey'.

• The Mel Gibson *Hamlet* (1990) – directed by Franco Zeffirelli, this showcased the man often thought of as an action star in the role of the prince, to widespread acclaim. Alan Bates played Claudius, Glenn Close was Gertrude and Helena Bonham Carter Ophelia. The veteran theatre and film director (and the man also behind the definitive *Romeo and Juliet*) made both the story and the setting compelling. Critics were very enthusiastic about the movie. Running time 130 minutes.

• The Kenneth Branagh *Hamlet* (1996) – with Branagh as Hamlet, Kate Winslet as Ophelia, Derek Jacobi as Claudius, this epic length (242 minutes) adaptation is spectacular and stimulating.

• The Almereyda *Hamlet* (2000) – with Ethan Hawke as the prince, Kyle MacLachlan as Claudius, Julia Stiles as Ophelia, this version relocates the story to modern day New York. Critics had mixed reactions to the film, but overall concluded that it failed. Bill Murray in the role of Polonius, for example, was singled out as a lamentable piece of miscasting. 112 minutes.

Overall, the two most satisfying are the Branagh *Hamlet* (for purists) and the Gibson *Hamlet* (for those who like an 'entertaining and energetic' version of the story). Here are reviews:

Quote

Hamlet has all the makings of a blockbuster: an all-star cast, grand-scale sets, a great history, 70 mm format, and Kenneth Branagh's pedigree behind it. A Shakespearean legend-in-the-making since he hit the screen in *Henry V*, Branagh has managed to meld the honesty of the stage with the braggadocio of Hollywood. And if what the critics are saying is true, he has finally hit the nail on the head with a Hamlet for all ages.

The Bard's greatest work was probably never meant for the screen, but Branagh's name assures that it will be done with both intelligence and intrigue. The changes in the script aren't too hard to understand; none of Shakespeare's original play, his longest, has been cut. In fact, all the changes are additions. Branagh has enlisted Tim Harvey, an Academy Award winning set designer, to work his wizardry with the scenery. Gone are the gray-scale, gloomy landscapes and castles that have haunted *Hamlet*'s past. Present are sweeping, dazzling halls and glittering, shocking costumes and hairdos.

The cast, of course, is equally impressive. Kate Winslet promises to be an endearing Ophelia; Julie Christie seems the right fit for Gertrude; Derek Jacobi has the range for Claudius; Charlton Heston, according to NYC feedback, is the best casting job in the lot as the Player King; and Billy Crystal and Robin Williams might provide some familiar faces. Branagh's performance in the title role should be worth the 240 minutes all by itself. (*Arts Weekender*, 1997)

Quote

This has been called by one movie critic "a visceral Hamlet" with Mel Gibson giving a gutsy or macho performance. Other versions by other actors I have seen play the character as tame and weak, not at all the powerful obsessed character I imagined in Shakespeare's play. Even Lawrence Olivier's *Hamlet* is meek – compared to Mel Gibson's, with Olivier giving little hint as to the torment of a man intent on avenging his father's death. The scenes with Ophelia, Gertrude, Polonius,and Claudius all require projection and expression of sincerely felt emotions to make the play work. The very talented cast that has Helen Bonham-Carter, Glenn Close, Ian Holm, and Alan Bates respectively in these roles compliment Gibson's performance admirably. Mel Gibson is a great actor who makes his roles believable and sincere....

Well directed with a beautiful landscape by Franco Zeffirelli, this version makes the play understanable to anyone who watches it....Those who complain that he took too much (erring) poetic license should know that many actors and directors do the same thing....In Zeffirelli's version, much of the wordy and unneeded material such as Hamlet's instruction to the players are removed, making what had been a 3 hour play into a two hour movie. All in all this is the best version I have ever seen. (Review on amazon.com)

Sample Essay

The tragedy of Hamlet is not a fatal flaw in the character of the prince. He is simply ill-suited to the role he must play.

Discuss.

Hamlet, Prince of Denmark, is not a man without flaws. Despite being well loved by the people of Denmark and much admired by Ophelia, he can be at times immensely, even whimsically, cruel. There is also a vindictive streak in his nature that sits oddly with the more charming side he often displays, a charm much enhanced by his wry, self-deprecating humour. However, none of his failings of character could be said to amount to a 'fatal flaw'. What impresses us most about him, and what gives his introverted musings such pathos, is that he is so clearly unsuited to the role he is called upon to play. He is reflective when others would be hasty, he is hesitant when they would plunge straight into action. He is squeamish when another man would be bold, resolute and bloody. Above all, he is moral in his deliberations when all around him are scheming and self-interested. It is the very virtues of Hamlet that threaten to undo him!

Focussed discussion of the topic's key ideas

We first become aware of Hamlet's private agonies at the same time that we see the vigour and self-possession of Claudius. In the second scene of Act 1 we witness the newly crowned king at the height of his powers, ready to move against his enemies and to anticipate any problems which might arise in court. Surrounded by sycophantic courtiers, and with his new wife beside him, he is the model of a man of action, annoyed by Hamlet's obvious melancholia. Indeed he seems positively discomfited, urging Hamlet to put aside such 'unmanly' displays of grief. What a weird contrast he makes with the silent man who broods through the first part of the scene! We can picture Hamlet in our mind's eye, in the sombre garb of mourning, making no comment, but watching all these proceedings with a jaundiced eye. Only the sly aside ('A little more than kin and less than kind'), alerts us to his

Early signs of Hamlet's problems

76

wary, suspicious nature.

Hamlet is troubled. His doubts about those around him, and indeed life itself, run deep. He is suspicious about the manner of his father's death. His mother's hasty marriage, rather more even than Claudius' ascension to the throne, causes him particular anguish. He cannot imagine what has happened to a world which seemed secure. Now it seems to be full of crafty actors. How could Gertrude profess undying love for her late husband and yet so quickly take a new one to her bed? From this point on Hamlet learns the bitter lesson that if he is to succeed in the world's terms then he must become more like the world. He will assume the roles needed to find out the truth of his father's death and play them to the hilt – whether it be the role of madman, of rejected lover or a logic-twisting schoolman. He can play them all.

Even when he thinks he is getting near the truth, however, Hamlet seems perversely reluctant to act. After 'The Murder of Gonzago' he is convinced Claudius is guilty, yet he does nothing. This failure to grasp the nettle will remain a mystery to us if we lose sight of the central moral dilemma of the play. Hamlet is a profoundly moral man unsure of how to act, because he is unsure of *the right course of action*. He must be assured, without a shadow of doubt, that Claudius is the wrong-doer and that nothing short of regicide will restore the kingdom, before he can take matters into his own hands. The words of his ghostly father cannot suffice. They may feed his suspicions but the identity of the ghost is too deliberately shrouded in mystery for it to seem absolute. Only when confronted by the self-evident guilt of Claudius in ordering his own death, does Hamlet begin to act with energy and resolve. Only when there is a kind of moral consistency established between the need to act and the justification for acting now, does Hamlet throw off the shackles and tackle his tormentor with a vengeance.

In Act 5 we witness the emergence of a 'new' Hamlet. Having returned from England with unanswerable proof of the king's evil plan to have him killed, he is like a man transformed. Everything which now happens to him seems to bear the stamp of a divine mandate. Even our indiscretions may serve us well, he informs Horatio. 'There's a divinity that shapes our ends/Rough-hew how we will', is the creed of this much changed man. What Hamlet is saying in effect is that the God's pre-ordained plan will achieve its perfect execution in him! If he is to die in pursuit of justice then that will be as God planned it. If he is to slay the usurper king, then

Reasons for his anguish

Hamlet's problem over taking action – why does he hesitate?

The new Hamlet who discovers certainty

that is also the way things were meant to be. Indeed if there is any madness in Hamlet it might well be megalomania! These are the words of prophets throughout the ages who have always *known* what is right, because God ordained it so!

That is why I argue that it is the very *virtue* of Hamlet which is his undoing. A lesser man, but a better politician (such as Claudius), would have acted with much more guile, allaying the suspicions of those around him, until he had learned the truth. Fortinbras would have destroyed without hesitation his father's enemies and slaughtered any who crossed his path. It is interesting that Hamlet professes great admiration for Fortinbras and even anoints him as the next king. He sees qualities in that hot-blooded young man which he feels he lacks.

Hamlet's problems not a 'flaw' but a virtue

Hamlet is an exceedingly complex man, an enigma we all would love to solve. But he is not a tragic figure in the classical sense of Greek tragedy. He is not a great man brought down by *one* flaw in his character. In some ways he is an eminently ordinary man, plagued by the kinds of doubts and uncertainties which beset us all. Above all else, he is a deeply moral person, ill-adapted to the guile, the forethought, the sheer cunning which marks a man of this world. His heart and his soul are more at peace in the contemplative world where a man seeks to know God's plan and to fit himself to it. Only when he achieves that certainty of knowledge does he assume the role of warrior. He becomes God's warrior, almost resolving the ancient paradox of the gentleman who would also be a Christian.

Conclusion returns to the topic

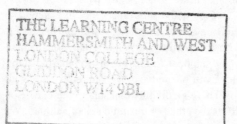

THE LEARNING CENTRE
HAMMERSMITH AND WEST
LONDON COLLEGE
GLIDDON ROAD
LONDON W14 9BL

Sample Essay Questions

1. 'Hamlet's tragedy is that he knows what he must do but he cannot do it. No one knows why.'

   Discuss.

2. 'What a noble mind is here o'erthrown,' says Ophelia.

   How 'mad' is Hamlet, in your opinion?

3. 'Good night, sweet Prince.
   And flights of angels sing thee to thy rest.'

   Horatio's brief eulogy affirms the essential nobility and goodness of Hamlet. Is this how you see him?

4. '*Hamlet* is a play about the pervasiveness of evil. In it, there are few innocents, and no winners.'

   Discuss.

5. The world of *Hamlet* is one of brutal men taking what they want by any means, while women are accused and reviled. It is a text that inadvertently exposes the poisonous nature of patriarchal societies.'

   Do you agree?

6. 'Let her paint an inch thick, to this favour she must come.'

   Hamlet is dominated by the theme of death.

   Discuss.

Titles in this series so far

A Good Scent from a Strange Mountain
A Man for All Seasons
Angela's Ashes
An Imaginary Life
Antigone
Away
Blade Runner
Breaker Morant
Briar Rose
Brilliant Lies
Cabaret
Cat's Eye
Cloudstreet
Cosi
Diving for Pearls
Educating Rita
Elli
Emma & Clueless
Falling
Fly Away Peter
Follow Your Heart
Frontline
Gattaca
Girl with a Pearl Earring
Going Home
Great Expectations
Hamlet
Hard Times
Henry Lawson's Stories
Highways to a War
I for Isobel
In Between
In Country
In the Lake of the Woods
King Lear
Letters from the Inside
Lives of Girls and Women
Looking for Alibrandi
Macbeth
Maestro
Medea
Montana 1948
My Brother Jack
My Left Foot
My Name is Asher Lev
My Place
Night
Nineteen Eighty-Four

No Great Mischief
Of Love and Shadows
Oedipus Rex
One True Thing
Only the Heart
Othello
Paper Nautilus
Pride and Prejudice
Rabbit-Proof Fence
Raw
Remembering Babylon
Schindler's List
Scission
Shakespeare in Love
Sometimes Gladness
Strictly Ballroom
Stolen
Summer of the Seventeenth Doll
The Accidental Tourist
The Bell Jar
The Blooding
The Brush-Off
The Chant of Jimmie Blacksmith
The Collector
The Crucible
The Divine Wind
The Freedom of the City
The Great Gatsby
The Handmaid's Tale
The Inheritors
The Life and Crimes of Harry Lavender
The Longest Memory
The Lost Salt Gift of Blood
The Kitchen God's Wife
The Outsider
The Player
The Riders
The Shipping News
The Wife of Martin Guerre
Things Fall Apart
Tirra Lirra by the River
Travels with my Aunt
We All Fall Down
What's Eating Gilbert Grape
Wild Cat Falling
Witness
Women of the Sun
Wrack